THE BALLET CALLED GISELLE

THE
BALLET CALLED
GISELLE

By

CYRIL W. BEAUMONT

One of a series of republications by

DANCE HORIZONS

1801 East 26th Street, Brooklyn, New York 11229

To

ALICIA MARKOVA AND ANTON DOLIN

Who have given new lustre to the
famous rôles of Giselle and Albrecht

and to

MY FRIENDS IN THE BALLET GUILD

Who share my affection for the ballet
called " Giselle."

This Second Edition is dedicated

To

OLGA SPESSIVTZEVA

Whose interpretation of Giselle will
long live in the memory of those who
were privileged to witness it.

Copyright 1969 by Cyril W. Beaumont.
This is an unabridged republication of the Second and Revised
Edition published in 1945 by Cyril W. Beaumont, London.
The typography used is that arranged by Mr. Beaumont.

Standard Book Number 87127-022-6
Library of Congress Catalog Card Number 72-77185
Printed in the United States of America

PREFACE

THE present work is, I believe, 'the first attempt, certainly in England, to study the evolution of a ballet from conception to realisation, and to follow it through its main phases of production. I have, moreover, endeavoured to view the ballet from both sides of the curtain, to consider and resolve some of the problems that confront both interpreters and producer, and to explain in detail to the spectator the action of the ballet.

It has often been lamented that it is difficult to discuss the choreography of a ballet because, unlike music, no score is readily available for the purpose of study. In the present case that need has been met, for I have included a simplified choreographic script or record of the greater part of the actual steps and mimed passages used in most contemporary versions of the ballet, as presented in this country. In defining the directions taken by the dancers I have made use of the Cecchetti system, which regards the stage as a square having eight imaginary fixed points. These are the four corners of the stage numbered 1, 2, 3, 4 beginning with the front left hand corner from the spectator's viewpoint and moving anti-clockwise, and the centres of each of the four sides of the stage, numbered respectively 5, 6, 7, 8. A plan for the use of the spectator will be found facing page 140.

I wish to record my grateful thanks to the Council of the Ballet Guild for so generously placing at my disposal a complete piano score of the music of *Giselle* and their choreographic score of the ballet, while Miss Molly Lake was kind enough to dance several of the passages for my express benefit. I am also indebted to several friends for various courtesies, in particular to Mr. Edwin Evans for help in elucidating certain musical terms in the Escudier notice, and to Miss P. Vanda, Miss A. E. Twydsen, Mr. T. G. G. Bolitho, Mr. Deryck Lynham, and Mr. W. B. Morris for the loan of illustrative material. In addition, Mr. Arnold Haskell and his publishers Messrs. B. T. Batsford courteously lent me from the former's book, *Ballet Panorama*, the photograph of Karsavina and Nijinsky in the Diaghilev production of *Giselle*.

Last, but by no means least, my friend Mr. Lionel Bradley did me the inestimable service of reading through the proofs, as well as placing at my disposal several items from his fine collection of ballet photographs.

CYRIL W. BEAUMONT

v

CONTENTS

PART ONE : HISTORICAL AND BIOGRAPHICAL

PART TWO : TECHNICAL AND CRITICAL

ILLUSTRATIONS

ILLUSTRATIONS

DUKE ROBERT SUMMONS THE DEAD NUNS FROM THEIR TOMBS. SCENE FROM
"ROBERT LE DIABLE"

From the engraving by Geiger

POSTER ANNOUNCING FIRST PERFORMANCE OF "GISELLE"

Coll.: Biblio. de l'Opéra, Paris

THÉOPHILE GAUTIER

From the etching by Bracquemond after the photograph by Nadar

JEAN CORALLI
From Saint-Léon's " La Stenochorégraphie"

JULES PERROT

From the lithograph by A. Lacauchie

CARLOTTA GRISI AND LUCIEN PETIPA IN "GISELLE," ACT I
From a contemporary lithograph

SCENE FROM "GISELLE," ACT II

From a lithograph published during the "eighteen-forties"

CARLOTTA GRISI IN "GISELLE," ACT II

From the lithograph by J. Brandard

MARTHA MURAVIEVA AS GISELLE (ACT II AND ACT I). REVIVAL AT OPERA, PARIS, 1863

THE INTERPRETERS OF HILARION AND THE PRINCE OF COURLAND IN "GISELLE,"
REVIVAL AT OPERA, PARIS, 1863

THAMAR KARSAVINA AS GISELLE IN " GISELLE," ACT I
At the time when she was a member of the Imperial Russian
Ballet. Note how her costume resembles that originally worn
by Carlotta Grisi

Photo : Dorothy Wilding

OLGA SPESSIVTZEVA IN THE MAD SCENE IN "GISELLE," ACT I

Photo : K. A. Fischer, St Petersburg

ANNA PAVLOVA AS GISELLE IN " GISELLE," ACT II

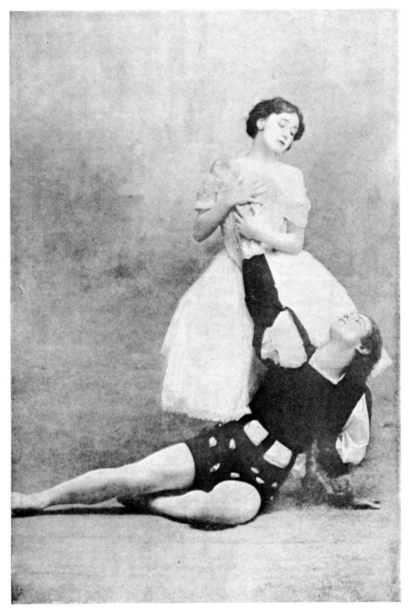

THAMAR KARSAVINA AND VASLAV NIJINSKY IN " GISELLE," ACT II
As presented by Les Ballets Russes de Serge Diaghilev, Paris, 1910

THE PHANTOM GISELLE BIDS ALBRECHT AN ETERNAL FAREWELL
From the lithograph by Célestin Nanteuil

ADOLPHE ADAM
*Lithograph from a drawing by Cauvin, based on a contemporary
photograph of the composer*

SCENE FROM "GISELLE," ACT I

From an engraving in "Les Beautés de l'Opéra," 1845

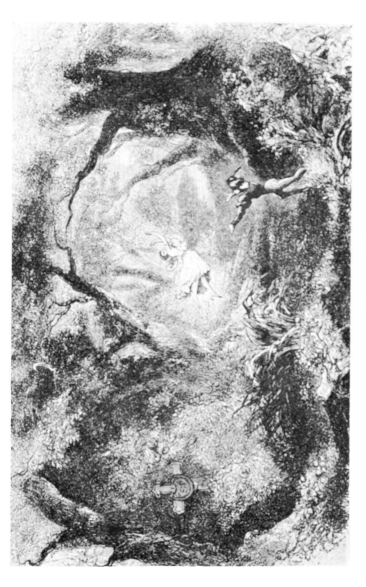

SCENE FROM "GISELLE," ACT II

From an engraving in "Les Beautés de l'Opéra," 1845

SETTING FOR PROPOSED PRODUCTION OF " GISELLE," ACT II

From the original water-colour painting by Hugh Stevenson

THE FLOATING WILI IN " GISELLE," ACT II

From Hopkins (Albert A.) " Magic : Stage Illusions and Scientific Diversions," 1897

SOME COSTUMES FOR EARLY PRODUCTIONS OF " GISELLE "
Above : Loys ; Giselle (Act I). *Below :* Huntsman ; Giselle (Act I)
The first three are by Paul Lormier for the original production of
1841, the fourth is by Alfred Albert for the revival of 1863 ; both
at the Opera, Paris

CARLOTTA GRISI AS GISELLE IN " GISELLE," ACT I
*From the engraving by H. Robinson after the painting by
A. E. Chalon, R.A.*

ALEXANDRE BENOIS. SOME COSTUMES FOR " GISELLE "
Designed for the revival at the Opera, Paris, 1924
Above : Wili ; Hilarion. *Below :* Giselle (Act I) ; Loys

SERGE LIFAR AS ALBRECHT IN " GISELLE," ACT II

LUCIEN PETIPA

From the water-colour painting by Prosper Dartiguenave

ADÈLE DUMILÂTRE AS MYRTHA IN " GISELLE," ACT II

From the lithograph by J. Bouvier

ALEXANDRA DANILOVA AS GISELLE IN " GISELLE," ACT I
As presented by the Ballet Russe de Monte Carlo, 1943

IGOR YOUSKEVICH AS LOYS IN " GISELLE," ACT I
As presented by the Ballet Russe de Monte Carlo, 1943

Photo : Baron

ALEXANDRA DANILOVA AS MYRTHA IN " GISELLE," ACT II

Photo : Wilensky, Buenos Aires

OLGA SPESSIVTZEVA AS GISELLE IN " GISELLE," ACT II

An unusual photograph, with the soft quality of a lithograph, which has captured something of the fragility and spirituality of that *ballerina's* interpretation.

ALICIA MARKOVA AND ANTON DOLIN IN OPENING SCENE FROM " GISELLE," ACT I

As presented by the Ballet Theatre, Metropolitan Opera House, New York, 1943

Action photo : Constantine, New York

DANCE OF THE VINE-DRESSERS : SCENE FROM " GISELLE," ACT I

As presented by the Ballet Theatre, Metropolitan Opera House, New York, 1943

Markova   Dolin

Action photo : Constantine, New York

GISELLE ENTERTAINS HER FRIENDS : SCENE FROM "GISELLE," ACT I

As presented by the Ballet Theatre, Metropolitan Opera House, New York, 1943

Markova   *Dolin*

Action photo : Constantine, New York

THE COLLAPSE OF GISELLE : SCENE FROM " GISELLE," ACT I
As presented by the Ballet Theatre, Metropolitan Opera House, New York, 1943
Markova   Dolin

Action photo : Bob Golby, New York

ALICIA MARKOVA AND ANTON DOLIN IN FINAL SCENE FROM " GISELLE," ACT I

As presented by the Ballet Theatre, Metropolitan Opera House, New York, 1943

Photo : Dorothy Wilding

OLGA SPESSIVTZEVA AND ANTON DOLIN IN " GISELLE," ACT I
As presented by the Camargo Society, Savoy Theatre, London, 1932

GISELLE LOSES HER REASON: SCENE FROM " GISELLE," ACT I

As presented by Les Ballets Russes de Monte Carlo, Theatre Royal, Drury Lane, London, 1938

Markova *Lifar*

Action photo : Merlyn Severn

GISELLE ABOUT TO THRUST THE SWORD IN HER SIDE : SCENE FROM " GISELLE," ACT I

As presented by Les' Ballets Russes de Monte Carlo, Theatre Royal, Drury Lane, London, 1938

Markova *Lifar*

SCENE FROM " GISELLE," ACT II : THE INVOCATION OF THE WILIS

As presented by the Sadler's Wells Ballet

Action photo : Baron

THE WILIS DANCE IN THE ENCHANTED GLADE

As presented by Les Ballets Russes de Monte Carlo, Theatre
Royal, Drury Lane, London, 1938

MYRTHA SUMMONS GISELLE FROM HER GRAVE TO BECOME A WILI : SCENE FROM " GISELLE," ACT II

As presented by Les Ballets Russes de Monte Carlo, Theatre Royal, Drury Lane, London, 1938

Danilova

Markova

SCENE FROM " GISELLE," ACT II

Margot Fonteyn beginning Giselle's *adage* which opens with a *développé à la seconde* followed by a *fouetté à l'arabesque*

MARGOT FONTEYN AS GISELLE IN " GISELLE," ACT II

Taken during the *grand jeté en diagonale*

Action photo : John T. Knight

ROBERT HELPMANN IN FINAL SCENE FROM " GISELLE," ACT II
As presented by the Sadler's Wells Ballet

OLGA SPESSIVTZEVA AS GISELLE IN " GISELLE," ACT II
As presented at the Opera, Paris, 1932

ALICIA MARKOVA AND ANTON DOLIN IN " GISELLE," ACT II
As presented by the Ballet Theatre, New York, 1943

Photo : *Alfredo Valente, New York*

ALICIA MARKOVA AND ANTON DOLIN IN " GISELLE," ACT II
As presented by the Ballet Theatre, New York, 1943

CHAPTER I

THE EVOLUTION OF THE ROMANTIC BALLET

THE year 1941 was an important date in the history of ballet, for it marked the centenary of the famous ballet, *Giselle*, first produced at the Opera, Paris, in 1841, and still danced to-day. Only one other work that is still being given can boast so proud a lineage, Dauberval's comedy-ballet, *La Fille Mal Gardée*, first presented at London[1] in 1786. But while *Giselle* has been performed more or less continuously in one State Theatre or another, and retained the greater part of its original music and a proportion of the original choreography, *La Fille Mal Gardée* has been subject to very occasional revival ; moreover, the theme alone has been preserved in its essentials, for both new music and new choreography have been imposed upon it.

That a ballet should have endured for over a hundred years, triumphantly surviving so many vicissitudes of taste and fashion, is a sufficient tribute to its popularity and wide appeal. There is no other ballet which in the short space of two acts offers such an immense range of expression to the *ballerina*, both as dancer and mime. Indeed, taken all in all, *Giselle* was and remains the supreme achievement of the Romantic Ballet.

To define Romanticism in its innumerable manifestations such as the gloomy landscape, picturesque outlaw, satanism, or the fatal woman, would be a considerable task. In essence it was a revolutionary movement directed against the domination of the arts by classic tradition and classic models. The actual word " romantic " was first applied in relation to literature, and occurs about the middle of the seventeenth century. It implied a work possessing the abnormal and fantastic qualities characteristic of the old romances. By the next century the word " romantic " became a synonym for " imaginative," and by the end of that century it came to mean any scene or event which arrested attention by its picturesqueness or fantastic quality, and so the adjective " romantic " related not only to the subject arousing emotion, but also to the mental and physical reactions themselves.

---

[1] There is still a measure of uncertainty as to whether the ballet was first given at London or at Bordeaux.

Among early examples of the new trend in literature may be mentioned Horace Walpole's *The Castle of Otranto* (1764), and Mrs. Radcliffe's *Mysteries of Udolpho* (1794) and *The Italian* (1797); it reached full development in the works of such writers as E. T. A. Hoffmann, H. de Balzac, Victor Hugo, and Théophile Gautier. The gospel of romanticism soon spread to art, for instance, the paintings of Delacroix, Géricault, and Boecklin; and to music, for example, the work of composers such as Weber, Berlioz, Schumann, Chopin, Liszt, and Wagner.

In Ballet, romanticism was the desire to overthrow those heroes of Greek and Roman mythology and history who had so long strutted the stage of the Paris Opera. Examine the titles of the ballets given there since its inception in 1672, and you will be surprised at the almost monotonous regularity with which they embody some classical or allegorical allusion. Here are some typical examples from a century of ballet : *Les Muses* (1703), *Les Amours de Mars et de Vénus* (1712), *Les Fêtes Grecques et Romaines* (1723), *Les Amours des Dieux* (1727), *Le Parnasse* (1729), *Les Romans* (1736), *Les Fêtes d'Hébé* (1739), *Pygmalion* (1748), *Deucalion et Pyrrha* (1755), *Céphale et Procris* (1775), *Medée et Jason* (1776), *Les Horaces* (1777).

The classic literatures of ancient Greece and Rome were regarded as an essential part of the education of polite society and their influence spread to every branch of the arts, both creative and decorative. Ballet, like opera, was essentially an entertainment for the aristocracy, and its early performances were confined to court circles. Even when Ballet migrated to the public theatre, its audiences were drawn mainly from the ranks of the nobility and the leisured classes.

The ballet of the eighteenth century was highly sophisticated and full of conventions. The costumes were rich and elaborate, and the carefully-dressed wigs, wide-skirted coats, panniered dresses, and high-heeled shoes did not make for either great ease or variety of movement. The ballets for the most part dealt with heroic themes or were pastorals in the manner of the fastidious shepherds and shepherdesses beloved of Watteau, Boucher, and Lancret. At first the ballets were little more than a succession of *tableaux vivants* accompanied by or interspersed with actual dancing. Elegant dancing and refined spectacle rather than plot were the prime considerations until 1760, when Noverre initiated the *ballet d'action*, in which the dancers not only sought to appear elegant, but also to make their movements expressive of a theme devised with a view to dramatic effect. To judge by contemporary illustrations of such ballets, the mimed scenes were little more than theatricalised conventional attitudes associated with different emotions. The ballets, however, continued to consist largely of those inevitable *chaconnes* and *menuets* designed to set off the dancers in a series of cold and formal measures.

Even when the Directory came into power with Citizen Buonaparte, the vogue for classicism persisted, because the new republican party wished to emulate the glories of the republics of ancient Greece and Rome. Moreover, the future Emperor Napoleon had steeped himself in the classics and saw himself as a new Cæsar.

In 1791 there was an important innovation in costume destined to exert considerable influence on the development of ballet technique. This occurred in connection with the opera *Corisandre*, by de Linières and Le Bailly, music by Langlé, presented at the Opera on March 8th, when Didelot, in the rôle of Zephyr, appeared in one of the dances wearing a transparent tunic.

At this period the audiences comprised an increasing proportion of the general public. Impelled into a new world of sudden and violent change, a new world to be built upon the novel and unfamiliar principles of liberty, equality, and fraternity, they tired of a spectacle in which they had no interest and which belonged to a detested age now past.

One of the first choreographers to be aware of this new attitude was a pupil of Noverre, Jean Bercher, professionally known as Dauberval, who, from 1785 to 1791 produced several ballets based on scenes of village life, not the artificial life of Marie Antoinette's dairy at Versailles, but the workaday existence of the peasantry. The best-known of these ballets was *La Fille Mal Gardée*, probably the first comedy-ballet, first performed in 1786.

This new approach was the precursor of the romantic movement in ballet. Some twenty years passed before this was reflected in the ballets at the Paris Opera where, thanks to Napoleon's reverence for classical literature, the gods of heroic legend and the warriors of ancient history continued to flourish, despite the growing simplification of ballet costume.

Note the titles, typical of the new urge towards democracy :

Nina ou la Folle par Amour (choreographer, Milon), 1813; *L'Épreuve Villageoise* (*c*. Milon), 1815; *Le Séducteur au Village* (*c*. Albert), 1818; *La Servante Justifiée* (*c*. Gardel), 1818; *La Somnambule* (*c*. Aumer), 1827. All these ballets were concerned with the life, grave or gay, of the common people, generally country folk, and this background of peasantry afforded opportunity for spirited dances by peasant girls and youths. So much importance was attached to such *divertissements* that quite often the best dancers in the company were not those who took the principal rôles, but those who danced the *pas seuls* or *pas de deux* in the village dances.

Side by side with this innovation came a new development provoked by Bernardin de Saint Pierre's celebrated romance, *Paul et Virginie*, a moving tale of slave life on a sugar plantation in the Ile de France. This inspired two ballets produced almost simultaneously in 1806: *Paul et Virginie*, with choreography by Pierre Gardel, performed at the Opera on June 25th, and *Les Deux Créoles*, with choreography by Jean Aumer, presented at the Théâtre de la Porte Saint-Martin, June 28th; both ballets included a *pas nègre*.

These two ballets revealed the possibilities of " local colour " and the opportunity now afforded to informed choreographers of including national dances. This " local colour," at first purely geographical, presently added to its palette the bright colours of history, of dances associated with great periods of the past. Now there were ballets which had either a geographical or historic dance interest, and even ballets which included both forms.

Here, for instance, are some ballets with geographical " local colour ": *Le Dieu et la Bayadère,* opera ballet with choreography by F. Taglioni (India), 1830; *Nathalie ou la Laitière Suisse, c.* F. Taglioni (Switzerland), 1832; *Les Mohicans, c.* Guerra (North America), 1837; *La Gitane, c.* F. Taglioni (Spain and Russia), 1838; *La Tarentule, c.* J. Coralli (Italy), 1839; *La Péri, c.* J. Coralli (Egypt), 1843; *Le Diable à Quatre, c.* Mazilier (Poland), 1845; *Jovita, c.* Mazilier (Mexico), 1853.

Here, too, are some ballets which include both geographical and historical " local colour ": *La Révolte au Sérail, c.* F. Taglioni (Granada under Moorish dominion), 1832; *La Gypsy, c.* Mazilier (Scotland, Charles II), 1839; *La Jolie Fille de Gand, c.* Albert (Belgium, seventeenth century), 1842; *La Esmeralda, c.* J. Perrot (France, Middle Ages), 1844; *Betty, c.* Mazilier (England, Charles II), 1846; *Paquita, c.* Mazilier (Spain during invasion by Napoleon), 1846; *Catarina, c.* J. Perrot (Italy, seventeenth century), 1846; *Oʐaî, c.* J. Coralli (South Seas, eighteenth century), 1847.

Almost concurrently with the discovery of "local colour" came the third stage in the evolution of the Romantic Ballet, the cult of the supernatural, which, already remarked in literature, was first introduced into ballet in 1831. November 21st of that year saw the production at the Opera of Meyerbeer's five-act opera, *Robert le Diable*, in the third act of which is a mimed scene with dances, in which Duke Robert visits the ruined abbey of St. Rosalie and by means of a mystic branch summons from their tombs the ghosts of departed nuns.

According to Dr. Véron,[1] then director of the Opera, the original plan was to produce the scene in accordance with classic tradition, but his assistant, Duponchel, to whom he had entrusted the artistic production, devised instead, with the help of the scene designer, Ciceri, an eerie scene in which white-veiled nuns led by Marie Taglioni emerged from their stone tombs in a ghostly dance. This accidental "spiritualisation" of the ballet must have made a deep impression upon the tenor, Adolphe Nourrit, who sang the rôle of Duke Robert, and also upon Taglioni's father, the choreographer Filippo Taglioni, who arranged the dances; for not long afterwards Nourrit offered Véron the scenario of a ballet, later called *La Sylphide* (1832), which he had based on Nodier's fantastic tale, *Trilby ou le Lutin d'Argaïl*. Nodier was famous for his romantic stories, which tell how the lives of mortals are affected by the visitations of elves and goblins. In 1821 Nodier had visited Scotland in company with Baron Taylor; doubtless *Trilby* was the result of that journey.

Dr. Véron was delighted with the proposed ballet, for, as he said, "the action was simple, easy to follow, and the end most touching."[1] He showed the synopsis to Taglioni and his daughter who were no less enthusiastic and eager to begin work on the ballet. It was decided to call the ballet *La Sylphide*, and Véron tells us that "the better to justify the title, numerous flights of sylphides were devised, and, above all, a circling flight."[2]

The new ballet was first performed on March 12th, 1832, and among the distinguished audience was Théophile Gautier, who, some nine years later, was to visualise and be part author of

[1] *Mémoires d'un Bourgeois de Paris,* 1854
[2] *Op. cit.,* 1854.

another ballet, *Giselle*, in which the Romantic Ballet came to full flower.

The effect of the new style of ballet—I refer to subject rather than to choreography—has been recorded by Gautier himself. "After *La Sylphide*," he says, "*Les Filets de Vulcain* and *Flore et Zéphire* were no longer possible ; the Opera was given over to gnomes, undines, salamanders, elves, nixes, wilis, peris—to all that strange and mysterious folk who lend themselves so marvellously to the fantasies of the *maître de ballet*. The twelve palaces in marble and gold of the Olympians were relegated to the dust of the store-rooms, and the scene-painters received orders only for romantic forests, valleys illumined by the pretty German moonlight reminiscent of Heinrich Heine's ballads. Pink-coloured tights always remained pink, because there could be no choreography without tights ; only the Greek cothurnus was exchanged for satin shoes. The new style led to a great abuse of white gauze, tulle, and tarlatan, the shades dissolved into mist by means of transparent dresses. White was the only colour used."[1]

What is the story of *La Sylphide* ? It is in two acts, the first of which takes place in a farmhouse in Scotland. James Reuben, a Scots peasant, asleep in a chair by the fireside, dreams of a charming vision, the Sylphide. Nearby sleeps another peasant, Gurn, who dreams of a lovely village girl, Effie, who is to be married to James that morning.

Effie enters with James's mother. Gurn offers the former the feathers of a heron he has killed. She thanks him, and seeing James still deep in thought, reproaches him for being sorrowful on their wedding-day. James protests his love and kisses her hand. The betrothed couple kneel to receive the blessings of James's mother, while Gurn turns away to hide his tears.

Effie's friends arrive and offer her presents. James draws near the great fireplace into which the Sylphide had vanished, only to meet an old hag called Madge. He bids her begone, but the girls entreat him to let her stay and tell their fortunes. She does so and tells Effie that it is Gurn and not James who loves her.

James's mother, accompanied by Effie's girl friends, escorts the bride to an upper room to prepare her for the ceremony. James, alone, is divided between Effie and the Sylphide. Suddenly he sees the latter standing on the window-ledge. She

[1] *Gautier (T.), Histoire de l'Art Dramatique, 1858-9. Vol. III, p. 225-6.*

confesses her love for him. When James tells her that he is betrothed to Effie, the Sylphide is in despair and declares that she will die. James in turn confesses his love for her. The Sylphide, overjoyed, urges him to go with her, but he refuses.

Gurn, a witness of this scene, hastens to tell Effie and her friends. James, alarmed, places the Sylphide in his chair and covers her with a plaid. Gurn returns with Effie, who raises the plaid, but the sprite has disappeared, and Effie reproves Gurn for his unjust accusation. Neighbouring villagers come to join in the festival; the old people drink, the young people dance.

James, distracted, forgets to invite his bride to dance; it is she who invites him. But always the pale Sylphide, visible only to her lover, flits in and out of the dancers, vainly pursued by James.

The dancing ceases. James takes off his ring and is about to exchange it with Effie's, when the Sylphide glides forward, seizes the ring, and takes the opportunity to induce him to go with her.

Effie is ready and James is called, but there is no answer. Gurn declares that he can see James flying towards the mountains with a young woman. Effie is heartbroken and everyone is indignant. Mother Reuben calms Effie while Gurn kneels at her feet.

The second act takes place in a forest with a cavern. Old Madge and some other witches are seen casting spells over a boiling cauldron, from which they take a spangled scarf of sinister purpose, then return it to the pot.

Now James enters to be joined by the Sylphide, who dances about him. She summons her sister daughters of the air, who dance about him. The Sylphide teases James with her sudden appearances and vanishings, so that he wishes he could compel her constant presence.

Old Madge comes out of the cavern. He asks her forgiveness for his rudeness, and, when she asks if he needs help, tells her of his trouble. She offers him the scarf and tells him that he has only to entwine it about the Sylphide, when her wings will fall off and she will be his for ever.

When the Sylphide returns he invests her with the fatal scarf. Her wings fall off as foretold, but she swoons to the ground— dead. Her sisters sadly descend from the skies, gather her in their arms, and bear her towards the tree-tops, while James kneels, stricken with remorse.

The silence of the forest is broken by the joyful ringing of bells. Through the trees can be seen a bridal procession. Gurn, triumphant, is leading to the altar Effie, already consoled.

I have described at length the plot of *La Sylphide* because, as we shall see later, *Giselle* owes something to its structure and subject. *La Sylphide* partakes of all four " colours " of the " romantic " palette—the first act embodies the life of ordinary folk, as opposed to gods and heroes, the geographical local colour of the Scottish highlands, and the historical colour of another age—perhaps the seventeenth century; the second act transports the spectator to the new world of supernatural visions.

La Sylphide also marks a revolution in stage costume. The female dancers of the First Empire wore high-waisted tunics, pleated to reveal the figure. There was even a female Sylphide, as witness the lithograph by Engelmann of Mlle. Brocard, complete with wings, in *La Mort de Tasse*, an opera in three acts with music by Garcia and dances by Coulon, presented at the Opera on February 7th, 1821. But the new dress of the new Sylphide, created by Eugène Lami alone or in collaboration with Taglioni herself, was designed not to *display* the lines of the body, but to *conceal* them by means of a milky haze.

The dress consisted of a tight-fitting bodice, leaving the neck and shoulders bare, bell-shaped skirt reaching midway between the knee and the ankle, pale pink tights and satin heelless shoes; the only adornments were a pale blue ribbon about the waist, a pair of tiny wings between the shoulder-blades, a posy at the breast, a pearl necklace and bracelet, and a garland of convolvuli to frame the hair. It is said that the actual colour of the dress was not white, but a faintly bluish tint to suggest the clouds which were the Sylphide's domain. It may be, but in the gaslight of the stage the costume appeared white.

Another innovation, this time a development of dance technique, was the use of *pointes*, not as a *tour de force*, but sparingly, fleetingly, as a kind of third plane, midway between the ground and actual flight in the air. This new method of progression could be used to suggest ineffable lightness or a moment of ecstasy. It is difficult to state when *pointes* were used for the first time, certainly not in this ballet, for there exists a lithograph by A. E. Chalon, dated 1831, which depicts Taglioni standing *sur la pointe* as Flore in *Flore et Zéphire*. Moreover, Didelot's famous pupil, A. Glushkovsky, declares that he saw the Russian *ballerina*, Avdotia Istomina, who appeared at St. Petersburg from 1815 to 1822 " dance on the very tips of her toes."[1] But it can be said, I think with truth, that, in *La Sylphide*, *pointes*[2] were first employed appropriately and to excellent effect.

[1] *Memoirs of the Great Choreographer C. L. Didelot* (*Pantheon and Repertory of the Russian stage*, 1851).

[2] Mr. George Chaffee, well known for his researches into the iconography of the Romantic Ballet, has found a lithograph (pub. Berthoud, London, 1821) of Mlle. Fanny Bias in *Flore et Zephyr*, in which the dancer is standing *sur les pointes*, presumably executing a *pas de bourrée en cinquième position*. (See *Dance Index*, September–December, 1943, which contains *The Romantic Ballet in London*, by George Chaffee.)

CHAPTER II

THE ORIGIN AND CONCEPTION OF " GISELLE "

A BALLET is a composite work. Ideally, it is the perfect fusion of the arts of music, painting, mime, and dancing, and, when there is a plot, as in *Giselle*, the author of the synopsis makes an equally important contribution. The first performance of *Giselle ou les Wilis*, to give the work its full title, a fantastic ballet in two acts, was announced for June 28th, 1841.

According to official announcements, those responsible for the various contributions were as follows : Book : Vernoy de Saint-Georges and Théophile Gautier. Music : Adolphe Adam. Scenery : Pierre Ciceri. Costumes : Paul Lormier. Choreography : Jean Coralli.

When a ballet achieves a resounding success, it is more than likely that the spectator will speculate on how the ballet originated. In the case of *Giselle* we are fortunate, for one of the chief contributors, certainly the original source of inspiration, the distinguished French author and critic, Théophile Gautier, has recorded in an article he contributed to *La Presse* how that ballet came into being.

This information, contained in a notice of the *première*, and playfully addressed to a brother poet, begins thus : " My dear Heinrich Heine, when reviewing, a few weeks ago, your fine book, *De l'Allemagne*,[1] I came across a charming passage—one has only to open the book at random—the place where you speak of elves in white dresses, whose hems are always damp ; of nixes who display their little satin feet on the ceiling of the nuptial chamber ; of snow-coloured Wilis who waltz pitilessly ; and of those delicious apparitions you have encountered in the Harz mountains and on the banks of the Ilse, in a mist softened by German moonlight ; and I involuntarily said to myself : ' Wouldn't this make a pretty ballet ? ' "[2]

What is this legend regarding the Wilis ? According to

---

[1] This work, written in French, first appeared in a Paris journal, *Europe Littéraire*, during 1833. In the same year it appeared in German under the title, *Zur Geschichte der neueren schönen Literatur in Deutschland*. The first French edition, called *De l'Allemagne*, was published in 1835.

[2] *Op. cit.*, Vol. II, p. 133.

Heine, it is of Slavonic tradition. The Wilis are affianced maidens who have died before their wedding-day, but are unable to rest peacefully in their graves, since they could not satisfy during life their passion for dancing. Hence at midnight they rise up and gather in bands on the highway, and lure any young man they meet to dance with them until he falls dead.

But is Heine's explanation of the legend the whole story? That the legend is of Slavonic origin is doubtless correct, for there is a Slav word *vila*, meaning a vampire, the plural is *vile*, and probably *wilis* is a Teutonic form of *vile*, for the " w " in German has a " v " sound. Curiously enough, Puccini's first opera, produced at Milan in 1884, is also based on the same legend, when the title assumes the Italian form—*Le Villi*.

However, to return to the story itself. Why should young betrothed women who have had the misfortune to die before their appointed wedding-day all be consumed with a passionate desire to dance, an ambition which, unsatisfied during their lifetime, is so forceful that it persists even after death, when, as spirits, they at last gratify that long-thwarted ambition by dancing from sunset to sunrise? Again, why should these young women haunt the earth in order to induce some hapless male, encountered purely by chance, to dance to his death? It seems a most unreasonable and heartless proceeding.

Most dictionaries and works of reference are silent on the subject of the Wilis, but Meyer's *Konversationslexikon* defines the Wiles or Wilis as a species of vampire consisting of the spirits of betrothed girls who have died as a result of their being jilted by faithless lovers. Here, certainly, is a far more logical explanation of the Wilis than that of Heine, for it not only provides a cause for the maidens' early demise, but affords a reasonable excuse for their bitter vengeance on the opposite sex.

What is the appearance of the Wilis and how do they dance? Heine tells us. " Attired in their bridal dresses, with garlands of flowers on their heads, and shining rings on their fingers, the Wilis dance in the moonlight like the Elves ; their faces, although white as snow, are beautiful in their youthfulness. They laugh with such a deceptive joy, they lure you so seductively, their expressions offer such sweet prospects, that these lifeless Bacchantes are irresistible."[1]

But to return to Gautier. Having visualised a ballet in two

[1] This passage is taken from that part of *De l'Allemagne* which deals with Elemental Spirits.,

parts, the second of which would illustrate the legend of the Wilis, he sought for a theme which would ensure the death of his heroine in the first part, so that she might appear as a Wili in the final episode. To this end he planned a first act suggested by the fate of the young Spanish girl in Victor Hugo's poem, "*Fantômes*,"[1] in his book, *Les Orientales.*

Gautier had an immense admiration for Hugo's poetry and, in pondering over the legend of the Wilis, no doubt the line, *Elle aimait trop le bal, c'est ce qui l'a tuée*, which might be rendered, *She was over fond of dancing and paid with her life*, leaped to his mind from its extraordinary coincidence of cause and effect. The poem tells of a young girl who, passionately fond of dancing, catches a fatal chill as she leaves the ballroom to return home, through her overheated body coming into contact with the cold breath of dawn.

"I had thought," Gautier tells us, "of making the first act consist of a mimed version of Victor Hugo's delightful poem. One would have seen a beautiful ballroom belonging to some prince; the candles would have been lighted, but the guests would not have arrived; the Wilis, attracted by the joy of dancing in a room glittering with crystal and gilding, would have shown themselves for a moment in the hope of adding to their number. The Queen of the Wilis would have touched the floor with her magic wand to fill the dancers' feet with an insatiable desire for contredanses, waltzes, galops, and mazurkas. The advent of the lords and ladies would have made them fly away like so many vague shadows. Giselle, having danced all that evening, excited by the magic floor and the desire to keep her lover from inviting other women to dance, would have been surprised by the cold dawn like the young Spanish girl, and the pale Queen of the Wilis, invisible to all, would have laid her icy hand on her heart."[2]

But when the proposed theme is examined critically, it is seen to be little more than a succession of dances with a single dramatic note at the end; there is an almost complete absence of action. In short, the theme is no more than an *idea* for a ballet, an idea which has still to be developed into an ordered drama, with its introduction, plot, and climax.

This was Gautier's first attempt at writing for the theatre, and, after reflection, he must have formed the conclusion that he needed skilled assistance, for, on going that same evening to

[1] Part III, 3rd verse.
[2] *Op. cit.*, Vol. II, pp. 137, 138.

the Opera and happening to meet Vernoy de Saint-Georges, a well-known librettiſt, he promptly imparted to him his idea and secured the promise of his aid. The synopsis, Gautier tells us, was accepted by the direƈtor, Léon Pillet, three days later.

In his notice of the *première* of *Giselle*, Gautier concludes his account of the firſt aƈt with the words : " There, my dear Heine, that is the story invented by M. de Saint-Georges to bring about the pretty death we needed."[1] The firſt aƈt then was clearly the work of Saint-Georges. Whether the second aƈt was the joint produƈt of Gautier and Saint-Georges, or whether the former did no more than suggeſt the dramatic possibilities of the Wilis, we do not know. But while the firſt aƈt is a competent but undistinguished piece of " ſtage carpentry," the second is a genuinely poetic conception which suggeſts that Gautier had a hand in it. There can be little doubt, however, that Saint-Georges collaborated, for all the chief charaƈters of the firſt aƈt—admittedly his creations—appear in the second.

Jules Henri Vernoy, Marquis de Saint-Georges (1801–1875) was a famous charaƈter in his day. His slender, immaculately-dressed figure, small, delicate features, smoothly-brushed hair parted at the side and adorned with little cluſters of curls at the ears, tiny moustache, and thin fringe of whisker running along the edge of the jaw, suggeſt an ariſtocratic dandy of the d'Orsay type. Saint-Georges had the same luxurious taſtes. His rooms were richly furnished with soft carpets, padded door-curtains, and muslin draperies, while portraits of women stood side by side with coſtly *objets d'art* and wax candles coloured blue, pink or green. He had a passion for the moſt exquisite perfumes, and when he went for a holiday by the sea he never entered the water without firſt emptying therein several bottles of the choiceſt *eau de cologne*.[2]

Yet, notwithſtanding his sybaritic taſtes, Saint-Georges was endowed with a fertile imagination and tireless pen. His firſt essay at writing was a novel, *Nuits Terribles*, published when he was only twenty. Then he turned his attention to the theatre ; *libretti* for comic operas and grand operas, synopses for ballets, followed in quick succession. Previous to *Giselle* he had already written the words for nine comic operas ; one grand opera, *La Reine de Chypre* (1841) ; and two ballets, *La Gipsy* (1839) and *Le Diable Amoureux* (1840). But these were no more than a token of what was to follow, for he was finally responsible,

[1] *Op. cit.*, Vol. II, p. 137.
[2] Boigne (Charles de), *Petits Mémoires de l'Opéra*, 1857.

wholly or in part, for the books of twelve ballets variously written in collaboration with Mazilier, Gautier, Albert, Perrot, Marie Taglioni, or Marius Petipa, and about eighty operas and comic operas, some written in collaboration, mainly with Eugène Scribe.

In plan, *Giselle* follows that of *La Sylphide*. The first act is concerned with simple village life, affording opportunity for picturesque peasant dances. The second act contains the supernatural element, the contest between mortal and immortal. The plot of the first act is likewise similar, the familiar situation being again employed. In *La Sylphide*, James, about to wed Effie, falls in love with the Sylphide ; while, in *Giselle*, Albrecht, already betrothed to Bathilde, is enamoured of Giselle. The setting of the second act, one of the chief features of which is Giselle's grave, would appear to be partly inspired by the tomb scene in *Robert le Diable*, just as Myrtha's magic sceptre of rosemary seems to be derived from Robert's mystic branch.

The next stage in the evolution of *Giselle* is a little puzzling. Since the director had already accepted the synopsis, one would have thought that he would have commissioned a composer to write the music and appointed a choreographer, unless Gautier and Saint-Georges had stipulated that they should select their collaborators.

Gautier had admired Grisi ever since he had seen her *début* in *Le Zingaro*, on February 28th, 1840, at the Théâtre de la Renaissance, Paris. Partly owing to the impression she made on this occasion, and perhaps still more as the result of pressure brought to bear on the director, Grisi secured a contract at the Opera as *sujet*. She made her *début* there on February 12th, 1841, in a *pas de deux* interpolated in Donizetti's *La Favorite*, her partner being Lucien Petipa. Gautier says of the new dancer : " She is possessed of a strength, lightness, suppleness, and originality which at once place her between Elssler and Taglioni. . . . Her success is complete and lasting. She has beauty, youth, and talent—an admirable combination."[1]

But Gautier not only admired the dancer, he was in love with the woman. Foreseeing her success in *Giselle*, and perhaps hoping to increase her esteem for him, he doubtless showed the synopsis of the new ballet to her husband, Perrot. It is easy to imagine how such a subject would have appealed to his lively imagination and sensitive feeling for dramatic situations.

[1] *Op. cit.*, Vol. II, p. 103.

Adolphe Adam, who was to compose the music of *Giselle*, tells us in his unpublished *Mémoires*,[1] that Léon Pillet suggested that Grisi should create the title-rôle in a recently completed ballet by Adam, *La Jolie Fille de Gand*, already in rehearsal, but " she found it a little long and for her first rôle desired a theme with more dancing. Perrot had just read me a very poetical synopsis by Théophile Gautier, *Giselle ou les Wilis*, a genuine ballet theme. I immediately seized it and, hurrying to Pillet, induced him to hold up *La Jolie Fille de Gand*. I undertook to do *Giselle* very quickly, pointing out to him that our major work would gain from the success which Carlotta would infallibly achieve in this one.

" I enjoyed composing the music. I was in a hurry, and that always stimulates my imagination. I was on very good terms with Perrot, with Carlotta, the work took shape as it were in my drawing-room."

Note that there is not a word about Coralli, who, according to the poster and programme, was solely responsible for the choreography of *Giselle*. Was it Adam who, having first persuaded Pillet to proceed with the immediate production of *Giselle*, next obtained from him the additional and invaluable concession that Perrot and not Coralli, the official choreographer to the Opera, should compose all the dances in which Grisi appeared, on the ground that no one knew better than he how to exploit her rare qualities as artist and dancer? It is certainly a possible and logical explanation, for Perrot, having established his wife at the Opera, and being very friendly with Adam, next hoped to obtain a contract for himself as dancer or, better still, as choreographer. An adept at divining the possibilities of a theme for ballet, he must early have realised the opportunities afforded by *Giselle* as a medium for his abilities as choreographer and as a vehicle for Grisi, whose professional welfare was his constant concern. The theme of *Giselle* is unique and ideal because its mainspring is *the dance*. The many strange and varied incidents which make up the story of the ballet are all the outcome of Giselle's passion for *the dance*.

Pillet, I think, saw the force of Adam's arguments, but having one *maître de ballet*, Coralli, already in his employ, he was not disposed to incur the additional expense of engaging another. I suggest, then, that Pillet, being well aware of Perrot's ambition to become choreographer to the Opera, turned that knowledge to his own advantage. He therefore allowed himself to be

[1] Quoted Pougin (Arthur), *Adolphe Adam*, 1877.

persuaded by Adam and accepted Perrot's services, which, in the event of the ballet's success, were to be rewarded not with hard cash, but with a vague promise of a possible future appointment as *maître de ballet*.

At this point it may be of interest to give some details of Coralli's career : I shall deal later and at length with Perrot. Jean Coralli Peracini, of Bolognese origin, was born at Paris on January 15th, 1779. He studied at the School of Ballet attached to the Opera, where he made his *début* on August 23rd, 1802, in *Les Mystères d'Isis*. His first essays in choreography were made at Vienna in 1800. From 1815 to 1822 he produced a number of ballets at Milan, London, and Marseille, among them being *La Folie de la Danse*, *L'Amour et l'Hymen au Village*, and *Armide*. He returned to Milan in 1824, where he produced *L'Union de Flore et Zéphire* (1824) for Paul, and *La Statue de Vénus* (1825) for Héberlé. The following year he became *maître de ballet* to the Théâtre de la Porte Saint-Martin, Paris, where he produced several ballets, including *La Neige*, *Le Mariage de Raison*, and *Les Artistes*.

In 1831 Coralli was appointed *maître de ballet* to the Opera, then under the direction of Dr. Véron, where he produced *L'Orgie* (1831), *La Tempête* (1834), *Le Diable Boiteux* (1836), *La Chatte métamorphosée en Femme* (1837), *La Tarentule* (1839), *Giselle* (1841), *La Péri* (1843), *Eucharis* (1844), and *Ozaï* (1847). The reception accorded these ballets was extremely varied. *La Chatte métamorphosée en Femme* was a complete failure, *La Tarentule* had a lukewarm welcome. On the other hand, *Le Diable Boiteux*, *Giselle*, and *La Péri* were triumphant successes, the first with Fanny Elssler, the second and third with Grisi.

How much of the success of these ballets was due to the choreography, and how much to the artist dancers associated with them, is difficult to say. A study of the themes of Coralli's ballets suggests that they contained a large proportion of mimed scenes, and that this was a characteristic of his ballets. As regards their purely dance aspect, contemporaries afford little or no information. Coralli retired from the Opera in 1848 and died at Paris on May 1st, 1854.

In view of these details, the reader may well inquire : what proportion of the original choreography of *Giselle* may be attributed to Perrot ? It is certainly curious that his name does not appear on either poster or programme even as *part* author of the choreography. What is the reason for this extraordinary omission ? Was it simply due to some regulation that Perrot, not being officially engaged as choreographer to the Opera, muſt preserve complete anonymity, or was there some other reason ? Whatever the cause, his participation was soon made public, as is proved by the following extracts from notices of the *première*.

" Apart from the authors cited in the programme . . . there is a fifth collaborator[1] unnamed—Perrot, Carlotta's husband and teacher, who has arranged all his wife's *pas* and scenes."[2] Again, " It is well to add, for the sake of fairness, since the bill makes no mention of it, that M. Perrot has himself arranged all his wife's *pas*, that is to say, he is the author of a good part of the new ballet."[3] Finally, there is the evidence of Adam's letter[4]

---

[1] A footnote on p. 168 of Vol. II of Lajarte's " Bibliothèque Musicale du Théâtre de l'Opéra " suggests the possibility of a third contributor to the choreography of *Giselle*—namely, Albert Decombe, better known as Albert. This footnote (to Coralli) asserts " La Registre de recettes porte constamment le nom d'Albert Decombe comme l'auteur des danses de ce ballet [that is *Giselle*] mais l'affiche et le livret portent le nom de Coralli." So far as I am aware, the whole case for Albert rests on these receipts, and while his participation is possible, I think it unlikely for the following reasons :

(1) Let us suppose that Albert was responsible for the choreography. He was in a very different position from Perrot, for Albert had not only been *premier danseur noble* at the Opera for the greater part of 1817–1831, he had also been *maître de ballet* from 1829 to 1831. Is it likely that he would have submitted quietly to such an injustice as the omission of all reference to his share ? Such a proceeding would not be in accordance with my experience of choreographers ! (2) At this period, Parisian journalists who specialized in the reporting of theatrical news were well acquainted with the details of impending productions and knew the inner history of them. If, then, more than one journalist, when reviewing the *première* of *Giselle*, was prompt to draw attention to the omission of Perrot's name and to make public his contribution to the choreography of the ballet, it seems very strange that, had Albert also been a contributor, none was willing to do a like service for him. (3) So far as my own experience goes, neither Théophile Gautier (part author of the scenario) nor Adolphe Adam (the composer of the music) makes the slightest reference to Albert, although, as they probably attended most of the rehearsals, they could hardly have failed to be aware of Albert's contribution, had he been a collaborator. (4) Finally, although I have read many contemporary memoirs of the Romantic Ballet, I have yet to come across any reference to Albert in connection with *Giselle*.

I suggest that the payments made to Albert were (1) for his preliminary work on *La Jolie Fille de Gand* but charged to *Giselle*, owing to some misunderstanding, or (2) that Albert received certain sums, charged to *Giselle* account by arrangement with the management, as a solatium for the postponement of his ballet, *La Jolie Fille de Gand*, in favour of the immediate production of *Giselle* ; or (3) that Albert may have taken some of Coralli's rehearsals when the *maître de ballet* was unable to be present owing to other matters claiming his attention, and received payment accordingly.

[2] *La France Musicale*, July 4, 1841.

[3] *La Revue Dramatique*, July 1, 1841.

[4] Given in full in Appendix to Lifar (Serge), *Ballet : Traditional to Modern*, 1938.

to Vernoy de Saint-Georges, describing the *première*, wherein he refers to Perrot as having had " a big finger in the pie."

It is difficult to eſtimate to what extent *Giselle*, as presented to-day, differs from the ballet as originally produced. The reader has only to examine the synopsis to see that several episodes have completely disappeared. I recall an illuminating remark made by the late Michel Fokine, when, about to leave England, he addressed his company after the *première* of a new ballet he had juſt produced in London. He urged them to remember everything he had taught them, for, without the conſtant supervision of the choreographer, there were few ballets which did not lose ten per cent. of their value after a week or two ; while, in six months' time, he added with a smile, he might be hard put to it to recognise his own composition. Judge, then, what may happen to a ballet produced a century ago, and subjeĉted to the frailty of human recolleĉtion, to the editing and adaptation by numerous choreographers, and to the demands of successive *ballerine* of widely divergent technical abilities !

But, viewing the ballet as presented to-day, it is almoſt impossible to resiſt the impression that the choreography is the work of more than one mind. For instance, the mimed scenes allotted to Hilarion, Albrecht, Wilfrid, and Berthe in the firſt aĉt are undiſtinguished ; they need genuine artiſts to lift them from the commonplace. Moreover, the episodes are ſtatic, no attempt has been made to fuse them with dancing. Now consider the " mad scene " in the firſt aĉt and the scenes between Giselle and Albrecht in the second aĉt, in which such varied emotions as love, tenderness, fear, and despair are conveyed in terms of dancing, dancing which is expressive in itself. It is difficult to believe that the same mind could range from the mediocre to the sublime.

Can the respeĉtive contributions of Perrot and Coralli be assigned with any degree of exaĉtitude ? I think not; at beſt we can but speculate. It is not unreasonable, however, to accept the contemporary ſtatement that Perrot " arranged all his wife's *pas* and scenes." It is very possible that he was also responsible for the episode in which Hilarion is trapped by the Wilis.[1] As to the balance, I think we may fairly assign to Coralli all the mimed scenes in the firſt aĉt associated with Hilarion, Albrecht, Wilfrid, and Berthe ; and, in the second aĉt, the entrance of the

---

[1] Note the similarity of structure between this scene and that of the capture of Medora in Perrot's revised version of Mazilier's *Le Corsaire* (see p. 37).

huntsmen, Hilarion's scene, the dances of Myrtha and the Wilis, and the scene (now omitted) between the peasants and the Wilis. Coralli's major contribution is certainly his dances for Myrtha and the Wilis, which reveal much imagination and thought. It is possible that the March of the Vinegatherers, originally an excuse for a spectacular procession—long since omitted—was also the work of Coralli, but it is well to remember that Perrot, too, had a flair for processions, as witness the famous Procession of Fools in his ballet, *Esmeralda*.

I attribute the dances of the Wilis to Coralli because Adam, in his letter to Saint-Georges, when describing the second act, observes, " There never has been anything so pretty in choreography as the groups of women which Coralli has arranged with so superior a skill."[1] Again, Gautier himself, when giving his impression of the Dances of the Wilis in the notice already mentioned, pays tribute to the assistance given by M. Coralli, who composed *pas*, groups, and attitudes of exquisite novelty and elegance."[2]

Giselle had its first performance on June 28th, 1841, as announced. It was preceded by the third act of Rossini's opera, *Moïse*. The cast of the ballet was as follows :

Albrecht, Duke of Silesia	- -	MM. L. Petipa
The Prince of Courland	- -	Quériau
Wilfrid, the Duke's squire	- -	E. Coralli
Hilarion, a game-keeper	- -	Simon
An Old Peasant	- - -	Petit
Bathilde, the Duke's fiancée	-	Mlles. Forster
Berthe, Giselle's mother	- -	Roland
Giselle, a peasant girl	- -	Carlotta Grisi
Myrtha, Queen of the Wilis	-	Dumilâtre

The new ballet achieved an outstanding success, " the greatest obtained by a ballet at the Opera," says a contemporary, " since *La Sylphide* of glorious and triumphant memory."[3] Moreover, in the same way as *La Sylphide*, the triumph of *Giselle* was confirmed by that most infallible of tokens, the homage of Dame Fashion : a well-known milliner, Mme. Lainné, offered her clients a new flower styled *Giselle*, while the *Journal des Femmes* records the important fact that Messrs. Poignée et Cie have brought out a new silky material called *le façonné Giselle*, or *figured Giselle*, said to be as pleasing as Mlle. Grisi herself.

[1] Lifar (Serge), *op. cit.*
[2] *Op. cit.*, Vol. II, p. 142.
[3] *Moniteur des Théâtres*, June 30th, 1841.

CHAPTER III

JULES JOSEPH PERROT was born at Lyon on August 18th, 1810. He was the son of the chief machinist to the Lyon theatres. The father seems to have early decided that his son should enter the dancing profession, for, when Jules was nine years old, he placed him in the care of a dancing-master, who was delighted at the unusual qualities of elevation and *ballon* displayed by his pupil.

At this time Lyon received a popular visitor in the person of Mazurier, the famous Polichinelle,[1] whose extraordinary leaps and postures aroused a furore wherever he appeared. Perrot went to see him in *Le Carnaval de Venise*, and came away resolved to do likewise. To this end he watched Mazurier's performance until he could imitate his every gesture and his every step. Then he obtained an engagement at the Théâtre des Celestins, where he exaggerated Mazurier's antics in a parody called *Le Petit Carnaval de Venise*, in which he achieved considerable success.

In 1820, at the early age of ten, he went to Paris, where he secured employment by day as a page-boy, while at night he often went on the stage as a super. In 1823 he made his *début* at the Gaîté, again in the character of Polichinelle. In another piece called *Sapajou* he took the part of a monkey, his miming being highly praised. In this rôle he found inspiration for his movements from watching the monkeys at the Jardin des Plantes. Revelling in his unusual agility and quickness he began to think of putting these qualities to a nobler purpose, in short, to renounce acrobatics for the art of classical ballet.

He studied under Auguste Vestris, and a little later appeared at the Théâtre de la Porte Saint-Martin, where he soon made himself a great favourite with his audiences. Bournonville, who had remarked Perrot at Vestris's class, says of Perrot in his Memoirs : " He was short of stature and of unusual build. Vestris took into account his unprepossessing appearance, and would not allow him to assume graceful attitudes. He said to him, ' Jump from place to place, but never give the public

---

[1] A French version of Mr. Punch.

28

time to study your person.'" This was the origin of the Perrot style, the conception of a restless being of rare lightness and elasticity, yet endowed with a strong personality.

Perrot inherited from Vestris all the perfection of technique which, in the eighteenth century, had attained its zenith in that great dancer, and which, at that period, enabled male dancing to dominate the leading exponents of the opposite sex. But, in accepting this legacy, Perrot did not become a slave to tradition; he had a mind of his own. His training as a Polichinelle had given him an excellent insight into stage values and theatrical effect, which he was to put to good service when later he turned choreographer.

But his ambition was to appear at the Opera, and, at last, in May, 1830, he appeared in a new dance interpolated in *La Muette de Portici*. The frequenters of the Opera were greatly surprised to see Perrot, whom they had previously regarded as a clever acrobat, make his *début* as an exponent of the pure school of classical ballet, and were considerably impressed by his extraordinary ease and lightness of movement, and his rare elevation.

In *Fernand Cortez* he partnered Marie Taglioni in a *pas de deux* which was highly praised. An eye-witness says of that occasion : " Each responded to the other. They moved together as though swayed by the same breath of wind ; they sank and rose as if moved by a common impulse. Perrot bounded about the Sylphide while she leant on clouds ; he floated about her like a powerful air-balloon ; together they plunged into pale mists ; they rose, one with her ineffable voluptuousness, the other with his temerity and audacity, both in the most melodious harmony."

Didelot's ballet, *Flore et Zéphire*, was revived to provide another vehicle for the combined arts of Taglioni and Perrot, and the excellent impression they made in that ballet was further strengthened by their appearances together in *Robert le Diable*, *Nathalie*, and *Ali Baba*. It would appear, however, that Taglioni, who wished to reign supreme in the world of elevation, became increasingly alarmed at the proximity of this dangerous rival, whose growing triumphs menaced her sovereignty, and eventually declined to appear with him. Partly as a result of this decision, and partly because he considered his services inadequately rewarded, Perrot left the Opera in 1835, and began a tour of the other principal centres of dance interest —Naples, London, Milan, Vienna, and Munich, at which cities he everywhere achieved the greatest success.

In 1836, Perrot went to the Teatro San Carlo, Naples, to take up his old part of Zephyr in *Flore et Zéphire*, so suited to his elevation. While there he noticed the work of a young dancer named Carlotta Grisi, who, although sustaining a purely minor rôle, greatly impressed him as to her future possibilities ; at this period she was scarcely seventeen. He took her under his care, personally supervised her dance studies, and fashioned her against the great day when he hoped to present her to the world as the new *ballerina*.

On April 12th, 1836, Grisi made a successful London *début* at the King's Theatre, in *Le Rossignol*, where she appeared with Perrot in a *pas de deux*.

Later in the same year Perrot and Grisi appeared at Vienna, where Perrot first tried his hand at the composition of a few short *divertissements*, such as *La Nymphe et le Papillon* and *Le Rendez-vous*. He also wrote and produced a ballet in seven scenes called *Kobold*, which was later revived at London. Being in daily contact with his pupil, it is not surprising that Perrot fell in love with her and induced her to become his wife. It would seem, though, that the young girl was swept off her feet by the dazzling prospects of such an alliance rather than by a genuine reciprocation of the affection her teacher bore her, for the union was not a happy one and the couple parted some seven years later.

From Vienna, Perrot and Grisi went to Munich, and then to Milan for the Coronation festivities. From Milan they moved to Naples. Grisi, having passed all these tests with honour, Perrot brought her to Paris, where they first appeared together at the Théâtre de la Renaissance on February 28th, 1840, in an opera ballet, *Le Zingaro*, in which Grisi both danced and sang. Gautier has left us a vivid picture of that triumph which is particularly valuable for its prose portrait of Perrot and its description of his manner of dancing.

"At last, here is something like a success ! The audience alone was the cause of it ; the spectators clapped their hands, stamped, and even threw bouquets on their own account ; they did everything which generally they leave to the management, like the great lords they are. Sauvage's words and Fontana's music had nothing to do with it ; Perrot's legs did it all. But what legs !

"Perrot is not handsome, he is extremely ugly. From the waist upwards he has the proportions of a tenor ; there is no need to say more ; but from the waist downwards he is delightful to look at. It hardly accords with modern views to discourse on a man's physical proportions; however, we cannot keep silent regarding Perrot's legs. You muŝt imagine that we are talking of some ŝtatue of the mime Bathyllus or of the aĉtor Paris lately discovered during an excavation of Nero's Gardens or at Herculaneum. The foot and knee-joints are unusually slender, and counter-balance the somewhat feminine roundness of contour of his legs; which are at once soft and ŝtrong, elegant and supple; the legs of the youth in red hose, who breaks the symbolic wand across his knee, in Raphael's painting, *The Marriage of the Virgin*, are in the same ŝtyle. Let us add that Perrot, in a coŝtume by Gavarni, has nothing of that feeble and inane manner which, as a rule, makes male dancers so tiresome; his success was assured before he had made a single ŝtep even; it was not difficult to recognise in the quiet agility, the perfeĉt rhythm, and the easy grace of the dancer's miming, Perrot the airy, Perrot the sylph, Perrot the male Taglioni! So, after the *grand pas*, the bravos burŝt out like thunder-claps!

"The *pas* is charming, the effeĉt is very pretty, and, contrary to cuŝtom, it has some meaning. . . . In it Perrot displays a perfeĉt grace, purity, and lightness; it is visible music, and, if the comparison be permitted, his legs sing very agreeably to the eye.

"These praises are the less to be doubted coming from us, since there is nothing we like so little as to see male dancers; a male dancer in anything else but charaĉter numbers and mimed parts has always seemed to us a species of monŝtrosity: up to the present we have only been able to put up with mazurkas, saltarellas, and cachucas. Perrot has vanquished our pre-judices. With the exception of Mabille and Petipa, the male dancers at the Opera only confirm our view that women alone should be included in a *corps de ballet*.

"Mme Carlotta Grisi seconds Perrot admirably; she knows how to dance, a rare quality; she has fire, but not enough originality; her dancing lacks diŝtinĉtion. . . ."[1]

Then came the success of *Giselle* in 1841, when Grisi made her triumphant *début* in the title-role and Perrot was highly praised for his known contribution to the choreography, notwith-ŝtanding that his name was omitted from the programme.

The following year *Giselle* was produced in London at Her Majesty's Theatre, with Grisi in her old part. During that season Perrot, in collaboration with Fanny Cerito, produced,

---

[1] *Op. cit.*, Vol. II, pp. 33–35.

on June 23rd, a new ballet in four scenes, *Alma ou la Fille du Feu*, in which Cerito played the title-rôle. The ballet achieved a great success, particularly the numbers called *Pas de Fascination* and *Pas de Trois*. Lumley, the director of the threatre, tells us in his *Reminiscences* that it was the talent displayed by Perrot in the composition and execution of the *Pas de Fascination* which inclined him to select that dancer to be his choreographer, while the *Pas de Trois* " raised to its height what the colder spirits of the time were pleased to call *Ceritomania*.[1] "

For the next six years Perrot was responsible for the production of the ballets at Her Majesty's Theatre, during which period he composed *Alma* (1842), *Ondine* (1843), *La Esmeralda* (1844), *Eoline* (1845), *Le Pas de Quatre* (1845), *Catarina* (1846), *Lalla Rookh* (1846), *Le Jugement de Paris* (1846), *Les Eléments* (1847), and *Les Quatre Saisons* (1848).

It is of interest to examine four of these ballets as examples of Perrot's conception of ballet. *Ondine* was first produced on June 22nd, 1843, with Cerito in the title-rôle. The theme, which owes something to Andersen's *The Mermaid*, is typical of the Romantic Ballet. Matteo, a young fisherman, is shortly to wed Giannina. Going to the sea-shore to catch a fish for his supper, he casts his net and captures a naiad called Ondine. She captivates him with her dancing and returning to the sea calls on him to follow. He is about to leap into the sea when he is restrained by some friends.

On returning to his cottage, Matteo tells his mother and Giannina of his adventures, which they dismiss as a day-dream. Suddenly the window blows open and Ondine enters. Matteo eagerly welcomes her, but when she bounds through the window and invites him to follow, he is held back by Giannina.

Matteo goes to sleep and Ondine reveals to him in a dream the beauties of life beneath the sea.

The following day Ondine lures Giannina beneath the water, when she is taken by naiads to the palace beneath the sea, while Ondine assumes the form of Giannina and induces Matteo to row her in his boat to his cottage.

The final scene is Giannina's bed-chamber when Ondine becomes conscious of the trials of mortality and cannot overcome an increasing sense of exhaustion. When it is time for her to accompany Matteo to the wedding ceremony, she can scarcely stand. But the Queen of the naiads restores Giannina to Matteo, and Ondine is borne to her home beneath the sea.

[1] *Reminiscences of the Opera*, 1864.

The great moment in this ballet was the *Pas de l'Ombre* in which Ondine, having assumed material form, sees her shadow which she vainly seeks to pursue.

La Esmeralda, first produced on March 9th, 1844, is based on Hugo's *Notre Dame de Paris*. Esmeralda, a street dancer, saves a young poet, Gringoire, who has been captured by Truands, by consenting to marry him. But Esmeralda is coveted by a Truand called Frollo, who later attempts to kidnap her, when she is rescued by Phœbus, a captain of archers, with whom she falls in love. He presents her with his sash, but when he asks for a kiss she takes to flight.

Next we see Esmeralda at home with her husband. She amuses herself by forming the name Phœbus by means of ivory letters. When Gringoire wishes to demonstrate his affection, he is roughly repulsed and retires to his room. At this moment Frollo enters and declares his passion, but she tells him that she loves only Phœbus. Frollo turns to see if the door of Gringoire's room is open and in that moment she escapes.

The next scene takes us to the splendid Gondelaurier mansion where Phœbus is about to be married to Fleur de Lys, the daughter of the house. Among the entertainers for the company is Esmeralda. Phœbus, recognising her, asks her to dance, when she displays such obvious pleasure that Fleur de Lys reproaches her lover. Furthermore, she observes that Esmeralda is wearing the sash she had embroidered for Phœbus. She snatches it from her and swoons to the ground. Esmeralda leaves with Gringoire, followed by Phœbus.

Phœbus and Esmeralda arrive at a tavern, where the former is attacked by Frollo, who stabs him to death and takes to flight. Esmeralda is arrested. Arrived at the prison she is condemned to death. As she is led to execution Gringoire bids her farewell. Frollo promises to save her if she will marry him, but she calls down the vengeance of heaven. At this moment Phœbus, who had only been slightly wounded, makes his appearance. He declares Esmeralda innocent and denounces Frollo, who is arrested in turn. But Frollo, enraged at the lovers' joy, attempts to stab Esmeralda, only to be struck down himself.

Esmeralda was highly praised both for the excellence of its dramatic construction and for the manner of its presentation, particularly the mimed episodes. When *Esmeralda* was performed at St. Petersburg in 1848, Elssler made a great success in the title-rôle. *Esmeralda* is one of the great dramatic ballets and is still included in the repertory of the Soviet Ballet.

C

Eoline ou la Dryade, first produced on March 8th, 1845, with Lucile Grahn in the title-rôle, is the story of a young girl—the offspring of a princely mortal and a wood-nymph—who, unknown to herself, becomes a dryad at nightfall. She is betrothed to a certain Count Edgar who has a rival in Rubezahl, Prince of the Gnomes. When the latter fails to win Eoline, he sets fire, on her wedding-day, to a mysterious oak tree with which her fate is linked, and as a result she dies.

One of the great successes in this ballet was the dance by which Perrot as Rubezahl endeavoured to subject Eoline to his will. There were several unusual effects in this ballet. For instance, the tree-trunks in the forest scene were given a semi-transparency so that the forms of the dancing dryads could be seen through them and thus acquire a charming suggestion of the supernatural.

The production of the *Pas de Quatre*, danced by Taglioni, Grisi, Cerito, and Grahn, and first performed on July 12th, 1845, is one of the great dates in the history of ballet, and was regarded by those privileged to see it as a choreographic masterpiece of the first order. It was remarkable not only for the beauty of the composition as a whole and for the perfect taste with which each dancer's particular resources were exploited to the full, but also because it was perhaps the first essay in pure dancing, for there was no theme. The critic of the *Illustrated London News* observes : " No description can render the exquisite, the almost ethereal, grace of movement and attitude of these great dancers, and those who have witnessed the scene, may boast of having once, at least, seen the perfection of dancing."[1]

At the close of the London season, Perrot was engaged at St. Petersburg, first as *premier danseur*, then in 1851 as *maître de ballet*. He made his *début* on October 19th, 1848, in a new ballet of his own composition, *Le Rêve du Peintre*.

In 1849 he went to Paris to produce *La Filleule des Fées* (October 8th), in two acts, seven scenes, and a prologue.

He returned to Russia, where he remained until 1858, during which period he produced eight new ballets : *Les Soucis du Maître de Ballet* (February, 1851), *La Guerre des Femmes, ou Les Amazones du IXe Siecle* (November, 1852), *Gazelda ou Les Tziganes* (November, 1853), *Marcobomba* (November, 1854), *La Statue du Marbre* (February, 1856), *La Débutante* (January, 1857), *L'Ile des Muets* (February, 1857), *Le Rose, la Violette et le Papillon* (October, 1857). He also revived many ballets, some of his

[1] July 19th.

34

own composition, some by other choreographers, for instance : *La Esmeralda* (December, 1848), *Catarina* (February, 1850), *La Filleule des Fées* (February, 1850), *Ondine* (January, 1851), *Le Diable à Quatre* (Mazilier, November, 1851), *Faust*[1] (February, 1854), *Armide* (Saint-Léon, November, 1855), *Le Corsaire* (Mazilier, January, 1858), and *Eoline* (November, 1858).

At St. Petersburg Perrot lived in a well-appointed flat in the Nevsky Prospect, and received many costly tokens of appreciation from the Tsar, Nicholas I. Perrot took to wife a pupil of the Imperial School for the Theatre, Capitoline Samovskaya, by whom he had two children. Having served some ten years in Russia, he began to tire of the quarrels and jealousies of some of his collaborators, and when offered a renewal of his contract, he was undecided whether to decline or accept until an incident occurred which impelled him to quit St. Petersburg for Paris. He was sitting one evening in his drawing-room with his wife and family, when a large mirror fell from the wall without any perceptible cause and crashed to the ground in pieces.

At Paris he revived acquaintance with many friends associated with the theatre and the arts, and lived the life of a well-to-do gentleman of leisure. But this did not prevent his paying frequent visits to the Opera to see Mlle. Théodore, the *professeur de danse*, giving her lessons, and sometimes he would take some classes himself. While on holiday at Paramé he died on August 29th, 1892.

*   *   *   *   *

Although Perrot was an admirable composer of purely abstract ballets and of ballets containing a considerable proportion of classical numbers, his prime interest was the dramatic ballet, the ballet which attempts to express a dramatic theme in terms of dancing and mime. In the dramatic type Perrot attempted an innovation which remains the ideal of all programme ballet, namely, to make the dancing expressive in itself.

He made use of six principal elements in his choreography : (i) *pas seuls* and *pas de deux*, (ii) the *divertissement*, (iii) mass dances, (iv) mime not strictly related to the music, (v) mime which followed the rhythm of the music, and (vi) expressive dancing or danced mime.

In the composition of a ballet, Perrot, although the greatest male dancer of his time, objected to the introduction of a dance

---

[1] Ballet in 3 acts and 7 scenes originally produced at the Teatro alla Scala, Milan, on February 12th, 1848, with Fanny Elssler as Marguerite.

purely as an opportunity for a display of virtuosity. If he did make use of virtuosity, it was always to ensure greater expressiveness, for he required all dances to stem from a situation, or to be explanatory of, or contributory to, the development of the action. Similarly, *pas de trois*, *pas de quatre*, and so on were not to be a mere diversion for the spectator ; there must be an interplay between the dancers to give the number point and character. Perrot always tried to make each person's dancing indicative of the stage personality of the individual represented. The same plan was followed in the case of *pas seuls* and *pas de deux*. The long *pas de deux* allotted to Giselle and Albrecht in the second act of *Giselle*, surcharged with an infinity of emotions, in which the dance continually reflects the changing situations, is a superb example of Perrot's application of his theories, and few dances in the history of ballet equal it for sustained poetry and expressiveness.

Perrot was unrivalled in his handling of crowd scenes and mass dances, which, as usual, sprang from some appropriate situation in the plot. Except when dealing with ballets concerned with supernatural elements, he disliked *ensembles* based on uniformity of movement. Each member of the *ensemble* was given different movements planned with a view to the combined effect, and accordingly as the *ensembles* were composed of the common people, soldiers, villagers, beggars, or gypsies, so Perrot sought to devise typical movements for each class of persons. He disregarded all contemporary theatrical conventions and did not hesitate to make his dancers turn their backs to the audience if this heightened the stage picture he wished to present. It is an effect which we have seen Fokine employ to perfection in his handling of the crowd scenes in *Petrouchka*.

Perrot was also fond of sharply contrasted simultaneous actions, or actions closely following one upon the other, which gave additional force to a dramatic situation. For instance, in his ballet *Faust*, the stage was divided into two scenes, one representing a room, the other a garden, the action in each being represented simultaneously. In *Esmeralda*, the riotous mediæval Feast of Fools is shown in the background, while in the foreground there is the dramatic scene between Esmeralda, Claude Frollo, and the Watchman. In an earlier scene in the ballet, Esmeralda tries to teach Gringoire to dance, hoping that he will eventually be able to partner her when she dances in the streets. He tries to imitate her movements, but only reveals his awkwardness.

In *La Filleule des Fées* two men are in love with a charming village maiden called Ysaure, who is under the protection of two good fairies. Her suitors are Prince Hugues and Alain, her foster-brother; it is the first she loves. A third fairy, jealous of Ysaure's beauty, declares that no man shall look upon her without losing his reason. Alain loses his reason and the Prince is made blind by the good fairies in order to save him from the same fate. Ysaure entreats the third fairy to restore her lover's sight. She agrees on condition that the Prince shall pick out Ysaure from among a number of young girls she will cause to be present. This piquant scene leads to a dance in which the groping, blinded Prince, guided solely by the impulse of his heart, seeks Ysaure among the band of girls, who attempt to mislead him by lavishing seductive caresses upon him, meanwhile the demented Alain continually passes to and fro, vainly searching for Ysaure.

There is another interesting effect in *Le Corsaire*, a ballet by Mazilier which Perrot revised and developed to a considerable extent. In the second scene of Act I, Conrad, a pirate chief, sits on a divan while his followers bring in a number of women captured in a recent raid. But he is only interested in one of them, a Greek girl called Medora, and bids his men remove the others. Conrad longs to embrace Medora, but although she has already fallen in love with the handsome pirate, she conceals her feelings. Hence, when Conrad wishes to take her in his arms, she repulses him. Then, when Conrad falls into a melancholy mood, she reveals her love by dancing. This dance is made so expressive that, as a result of the interplay between the two persons, the scene continually increases in intensity.

In another episode, Conrad's men revolt against their leader because, preoccupied with his passion for Medora, he ignores their clamour for action. They attack Conrad, who falls unconscious. He is discovered by Medora, who vainly summons help. When she attempts to escape, her way is barred by one of the rebels. She then dashes to the opposite side of the stage, to be similarly repulsed. This movement is repeated four times. Finally she decides to attack the pirates. She strikes at one with her dagger, then, exhausted, swoons and falls into the arms of her triumphant enemies.

The majority of Perrot's ballets have realistic themes of the picturesque type, and it is interesting to note that they frequently follow the growing democratic tendency in social life. Hence he often contrives situations based on the conflict between the people and the aristocracy. For instance, in *La Esmeralda*, Esmeralda, a girl who earns her livelihood by dancing in the streets, is pursued by the aristocratic officer, Phœbus. In *Catarina*, the hard life of the hunted bandits who inhabit the hills of the Abruzzi is contrasted with that of the aristocracy living in luxurious palaces in Rome. Sometimes, too, the aristocrat is satirised by presenting her as a helpless being when removed from her normal surroundings. This human situation is very effectively exploited in Perrot's version of Mazilier's *Le Diable à Quatre*, when, by fairy intervention, an indolent, overbearing Countess is forced to take the place of a basket-maker's wife, the transposition being unknown to the husband, whose real wife temporarily becomes the Countess. This juxta-position results in a variety of situations full of drama and humour.

Perhaps the best summing up of Perrot's contribution to the ballet is contained in a contemporary appreciation of his work by R. Zotov, the critic of the *Northern Bee*. " Up to the present we have asked of ballet no more than graceful poses, *plastique*, lightness, speed, and vigour. Now we see danced action ; every movement reveals a mind and a heart, every movement expresses some emotion ; every glance is related to the development of the theme. This is a new discovery in the domain of choreography."

The name of Jules Perrot is entitled to a high place in the annals of the dance, nevertheless, apart from his association with the famous *Pas de Quatre* of 1845, Perrot's career and achievements are little known to the average dance student. Yet he was the greatest male dancer of his time since Vestris, and remained unrivalled until the advent of Nijinsky, while, as choreographer and innovator, he was to the nineteenth century, what Fokine was to the present age.

CHAPTER IV

THE BOOK[1] OF " GISELLE "

ACT ONE

THE scene represents a pleasant valley in Germany. In the distance are vine-clad hills, across which runs a steep path leading into the valley.

SCENE I

This represents the vintage on the Thuringian Hills. Day is just breaking. The vine-dressers withdraw to fetch more grapes.

SCENE II

Hilarion enters and looks about him as if seeking someone; then he lovingly points to Giselle's cottage and angrily indicates that of Loys, which is his rival's home. If Hilarion ever has the opportunity to revenge himself upon him he will gladly seize it. The door of Loys's cottage opens mysteriously. Hilarion conceals himself to observe what is about to happen.

SCENE III

The young Duke Albrecht of Silesia, disguised in humble clothes and having assumed the name of Loys, comes out of his dwelling, accompanied by his squire Wilfrid. The latter seems to persuade him to abandon some secret project, but Loys is obstinate. He points to Giselle's cottage, that lowly roof that shelters the object of his love. He commands Wilfrid to leave him. Wilfrid still hesitates, but, at a peremptory gesture from his master, he salutes him with respect and withdraws.

Hilarion is stupefied to see a fine lord like Wilfrid display such regard for a simple peasant like his rival. He appears to conceive suspicions which he will clear up later.

---

[1] The text which follows is my own translation of the original published " book " of the ballet, entitled " *Giselle ou les Wilis*," *ballet-fantastique en deux actes, pdr MM. de Saint-Georges, Théophile Gautier, et Coraly*, pp. 19. Paris, 1841.

SCENE IV

Loys, or rather Albrecht, goes towards Giselle's cottage and knocks softly at the door. Hilarion remains concealed. Soon, Giselle comes out and runs into her lover's arms. Mutual transport and delight of the two young people. Giselle relates her dream to Loys. She was jealous of a beautiful lady whom Loys loved in preference to herself. Loys, troubled, reassures her ; he loves Giselle, and will never love anyone else. " If you deceived me," the young girl tells him, " I should die ; I feel it." She presses her hand to her heart as if to show him how often it aches. Loys calms her with loving caresses.

She gathers daisies, from which she picks the petals to be convinced of Loys's love. The test succeeds and she falls into her lover's arms. Hilarion, no longer able to contain himself, runs towards Giselle and reproaches her with her conduct. He was there and saw everything.

" Well, what does it matter ? " gaily replies Giselle. " I'm not ashamed of it. I love him and shall never love anyone else." Then she abruptly turns her back on Hilarion, laughing at his expense, while Loys pushes him away and threatens him with his anger if he does not cease making love to Giselle. " Very well," says Hilarion, with a threatening gesture, " we shall see what happens later."

SCENE V

A band of peasant girls comes to fetch Giselle for the vintage. Day has dawned and it is time to depart, but Giselle, passionately fond of dancing and pleasure, delays her companions. After Loys, she loves dancing more than anything else in the world. She proposes to the young girls that they shall amuse themselves instead of going to work. At first she dances alone to convince them. Her gaiety, her joyous ardour, her lively and seductive steps, in which she expresses her affection for Loys, are soon imitated by the other girls. Baskets, bundles, and tools are cast away, and, thanks to Giselle, the dance soon becomes a mad revel. Then Berthe, Giselle's mother, emerges from the cottage.

SCENE VI

" You will always dance then," she says to Giselle, " night

and day . . . it's an absolute passion . . . and this, instead of working in the vineyards or doing the housework."

" She dances so well," says Loys to Berthe.

" It's my one enjoyment," replies Giselle, " just as he," she adds, pointing to Loys, " is my only happiness ! "

" Bah ! " says Berthe, " I'm sure that if this little madcap were to die she would become a Wili and dance after her death, like all girls who are too fond of dancing."

" What do you mean ? " cry the frightened girls as they press close to one another.

Then Berthe, to lugubrious music, seems to depict an apparition of dead people returning to the world and dancing together. The terror of the villagers is at its height. Giselle alone laughs and gaily replies to her mother that she is incorrigible, and that, dead or alive, she will dance always.

" Nevertheless," adds Berthe, " it's not good for you . . . it will affect your health, perhaps even your life ! "

" She's very delicate," she tells Loys, " if she were to become over-tired or too excited, it might be the death of her ; the doctor told her that dancing may do her harm."

Loys, troubled by this confidence, reassures the good woman, and Giselle, taking Loys's hand, presses it to her heart and seems to say that with him she has nothing to fear.

A hunting call is heard in the distance. Loys, uneasy at the sound, quickly gives the signal for departure to the vineyards, and drives the girls away ; while Giselle, forced to return to the cottage with her mother, blows a farewell kiss to Loys, who goes away, followed by everybody.

Scene VII

No sooner does Hilarion find himself alone than he explains his project. He wishes at all costs to discover his rival's secret, to find out who he is. Making sure that he is unobserved, he furtively enters Loys's cottage. At this moment the calls sound nearer and huntsmen and whippers-in appear on the hillside.

Scene VIII

Soon the Prince of Courland and his daughter Bathilde appear riding on horseback, accompanied by a numerous following of lords and ladies, and falconers with falcons on their wrists. The heat of the day is overpowering and they seek a favourable place for repose. A huntsman points out Berthe's cottage to the Prince. He knocks at the door and Giselle appears on the threshold, followed by her mother. The Prince gaily requests the vine-dresser's hospitality. She begs him to enter her cottage, although it is a poor place in which to receive so fine a lord. During this time Bathilde goes to Giselle and, glancing at her, finds her charming. Giselle exerts herself to the utmost to do the honours of her modest dwelling ; she begs Bathilde to be seated, and offers her fruit and milk. Bathilde, charmed with Giselle's grace, takes a gold chain from her neck and clasps it round that of the young girl, who is both proud and shy at this gift.

Bathilde questions Giselle on her work and pleasures.

She is happy and has no sorrows or cares ; in the morning she works, in the evening she dances. " Yes," says Berthe to Bathilde, " dancing above all, that is her passion."

Bathilde smiles and asks Giselle if her heart has spoken, if she is in love with anyone. " Oh, yes," cries the young girl, indicating Loys's cottage. " He who lives there is my lover, my betrothed. I should die if he did not love me any more." Bathilde seems to take great interest in the young girl—their case is similar, for she, too, is going to be married to a young and handsome lord. She will give a dowry to Giselle, who seems to please her more and more. Bathilde wishes to see Giselle's *fiancé*, and re-enters the cottage, followed by her father and Berthe, while Giselle goes to fetch Loys.

The Prince signs to his followers to continue the hunt ; he is tired and wishes to rest a little while. He will sound his horn when he desires to recall them.

Hilarion, who appears at the door of Loys's cottage, sees the Prince and overhears the commands which he gives. The Prince and his daughter go into Berthe's cottage.

SCENE IX

While Giselle looks up the road to see if she can perceive her lover, Hilarion comes out of Loys's cottage bearing a sword and a nobleman's mantle. At last he knows his rival ; he is a great lord. Now he is sure he is a seducer in disguise. He can now take his revenge, and wishes to confront Loys in the presence of Giselle and all the villagers. He conceals the sword in a bush, waiting until all the vine-dressers are gathered for the east.

42

Scene X

Loys appears in the distance. He looks uneasily about him to make certain that the hunt is far away. Giselle perceives him and flies to his arms. At this moment joyful music is heard.

Scene XI

A march begins. The vintage is over. Slowly there comes into view a wagon decorated with palms and flowers, followed by all the girls and youths of the valley, with their baskets filled with grapes. A little figure of Bacchus sitting astride a cask is borne in triumph, according to an ancient local custom. Giselle is surrounded. She is declared Queen of the Vintage and crowned with flowers and palms. Loys is more than ever in love with the pretty vine-dresser. The villagers soon give themselves up to the most extravagant expressions of joy.

The vintage festival must be celebrated. Giselle can now indulge her favourite pastime; she leads Loys away from the midst of a group of vine-dressers and dances with him, surrounded by all the villagers, who soon join in with the young couple, whose dance ends with a kiss which Loys bestows on Giselle. On seeing this, the envious Hilarion's pent-up jealousy can no longer be controlled. He leaps into the midst of the crowd and tells Giselle that Loys is a deceiver, a seducer, a nobleman in disguise! Giselle, at first alarmed, tells Hilarion that he does not know what he is saying; that he has been dreaming. " Oh, I've been dreaming, have I ? " continues the gamekeeper. " Well, then, see for yourself," he cries, displaying to the villagers' gaze the sword and mantle of Loys. " These are what I found in his hut—proof enough, I should think." Albrecht, enraged, dashes at Hilarion, who takes shelter behind the villagers.

Giselle, overcome with surprise and sadness at this revelation, seems to receive a terrible blow and leans against a tree, breathless and on the verge of collapse. The villagers remain dumbfounded. Loys, or rather Albrecht, runs to Giselle, and, still convinced that he can deny his rank, tries to restore her confidence and calm her with tender avowals. " It is all a mistake," he says ; " he is only Loys, a humble peasant, her lover, her betrothed."

The poor girl asks nothing better than to believe him. Already hope seems to be reborn in her heart. She allows herself to go, happy and confident, to the arms of the perfidious Albrecht ;

while Hilarion, following up his vengeance and remembering the Prince's order to his suite, to return at the sound of his hunting-horn, seizes one belonging to a nobleman, which is attached to a tree, and blows it with all his might. At this signal the hunting-party come running up and the Prince emerges from Berthe's cottage. Hilarion points out to the Prince's suite Albrecht on his knees before Giselle, and each, on recognising the young Duke, overwhelms him with marks of respect. Giselle, perceiving this, can no longer doubt Albrecht's exalted station and her own misfortune.

SCENE XII

The Prince goes forward in his turn, recognises Albrecht, and, discovering him so, asks the meaning of his strange conduct and the purpose of the costume he is wearing.

Albrecht rises, stupefied and distracted by this encounter.

Giselle has seen all. She is now convinced of this new betrayal on the part of the one she loves, her grief is boundless; she seems to make an effort to control herself and avoids Albrecht with a sense of aversion and horror. Then, as though overwhelmed by this new blow, she runs towards her cottage and falls into the arms of her mother, who at this moment comes out, accompanied by Bathilde.

SCENE XIII

Bathilde goes quickly towards Giselle and questions her with touching interest regarding her manifest distress. Her sole reply is to point out Albrecht, oppressed and confounded.

"What do I see?" says Bathilde, "the Duke in such a guise! But it is he I am to marry. He is my *fiancé*," she adds, showing the engagement ring on her finger.

Albrecht goes to Bathilde and vainly attempts to prevent her uttering this terrible avowal; but Giselle has heard everything, understood all. The deepest horror is depicted on the unfortunate girl's features; her brain begins to reel, a horrible and sombre delirium seizes her as she sees herself jilted, lost, dishonoured. Her mind wanders, she bursts into tears, then she gives a nervous laugh. She takes Albrecht's hand, places it on her heart, and soon pushes it away in fear. She seizes Albrecht's sword still lying on the ground, and at first plays mechanically with the weapon, then she falls on its sharp point just as her mother leaps upon her and drags it away. The poor child recalls her love of dancing; she imagines she hears the melody of her dance with Albrecht; she darts forward and begins to dance forcefully and passionately. But so many sudden griefs, so many cruel shocks, added to this final effort, have at last exhausted her failing strength. Life is about to forsake her, her mother takes her in her arms, a last sigh escapes from poor Giselle's heart; she throws a sad, despairing glance at Albrecht; then her eyes close for ever.

Bathilde, kind and generous, sheds tears. Albrecht, forgetting everything, tries to revive Giselle with burning caresses. He places his hand on the young girl's heart and finds to his horror that it has ceased to beat. He seizes his sword to kill himself, but the Prince stops Albrecht and disarms him. Berthe supports her unfortunate daughter's body, while Albrecht is led away, crazed with despair and love.

The villagers, noblemen, and all the members of the hunting party close round and complete this sad picture.

ACT TWO

The setting depicts a forest on the banks of a pool. A damp and chilly spot with intermingled rushes, reeds, clumps of wild flowers, and water plants. Birch trees, aspens, and weeping willows droop their pale foliage. To the left, beneath a cypress, stands a white marble cross, carved with the name—Giselle. The tomb is almost hidden beneath dense masses of grass and wild flowers. The bluish gleam of a very bright moon gives a cold and misty appearance to the scene.

SCENE I

Some gamekeepers arrive by different paths in the forest. They appear to be seeking a suitable observation post and are about to decide on the bank of the pool when Hilarion runs up.

SCENE II

Hilarion evinces the liveliest fear on learning of his companion's plan. "It is an evil spot," he tells them, "where the Wilis dance their nightly round." He shows them the tomb of Giselle, Giselle who was always dancing. He points out the crown of vine-leaves which she wore on her brow during the festival, and which is attached to the marble cross. At this moment, midnight is heard striking in the distance : it is the gloomy hour at which, according to local legend, the Wilis foregather in their ballroom.

Hilarion and his companions are terror-stricken on hearing the clock strike. Trembling, they look about them as though expecting the apparition of the airy phantoms. "Let us flee," says Hilarion, "the Wilis are pitiless ; they seize upon wayfarers and force them to dance until their victims die of weariness or are engulfed in the lake you see here."

Fantastic music is heard. The gamekeepers grow pale, falter, and flee in all directions with every sign of fear, pursued by will-o'-the-wisps, who appear from all sides.

A sheaf of bullrushes slowly opens and from the depths of the humid vegetation darts a pale, transparent shade, the airy Myrtha, Queen of the Wilis. She sheds a mystic radiance which suddenly illumines the forest, piercing the shades of night. This light is ever present when the Wilis appear. On Myrtha's white shoulders tremble and flutter the diaphanous wings with which the Wili can envelop herself as though in a gauzy veil.

This intangible apparition cannot remain stationary, and darting now on a clump of flowers, now on a branch of willow, she bounds here and there, traversing and seeming to explore her tiny empire, of which she nightly resumes possession. She bathes in the waters of the lake, then suspends herself from the willow-branches and swings on them.

After a solo dance she plucks a branch of rosemary, with which she touches in turn every plant, every bush, and every clump of foliage.

SCENE IV

Hardly has the flowery sceptre of the Queen of the Wilis rested on an object than the plant, flower, or bush opens to set free another Wili, who in her turn joins the graceful group which surrounds Myrtha, like bees about their queen. The last-named, on hearing the azure wings of her subjects, signs to them to dance. Several Wilis successively appear before their sovereign.

First Moyna, the *odalisque*, executing an oriental dance ; next, Zulma, the *bayadère*, displaying her Indian poses ; then two Frenchwomen, dancing a kind of fantastic menuet ; and afterwards some German women, waltzing among themselves. Finally, they are joined by the whole band of Wilis, all of whom perished from having loved dancing too well, or passed away too early in life to gratify sufficiently that foolish passion, to which they appear to surrender themselves with fury in their graceful metamorphosis.

Presently, at a sign from the Queen, the fantastic ball ceases. She informs her subjects of the arrival of a new sister. All range themselves about the Queen.

SCENE V

A bright and vivid ray of moonlight outlines Giselle's tomb, and the flowers which cover it rise erect on their tall stems, as if to make way for the pale being they cover.

Giselle appears swathed in her thin shroud. She goes towards Myrtha, who touches her with her branch of rosemary; the shroud falls off and Giselle is changed into a Wili. Her wings grow and unfold. Her feet skim the ground. She dances, or rather darts, into the air like her graceful sisters, joyfully recalling and sketching the steps which she danced in the first act, before her death. A distant clamour is heard. The Wilis disperse and hide in the rushes.

Some village youths, returning from a festival at a neighbouring hamlet and led by an old peasant, gaily cross the scene. They are about to depart when strange music is heard, the dance melody of the Wilis. The villagers, in spite of themselves, are seized with a strange passion for dancing. The Wilis soon surround them, twine about them, and fascinate them with their sensuous poses.

Each of the Wilis attempts to detain the villagers, trying to please with steps appropriate to her nationality. The affected wayfarers are about to succumb to their wiles, to dance and die, when the old peasant, horror-stricken, dashes into their midst, tells them of the danger they run, and rescues them all, pursued by the Wilis, furious at the sight of their prey escaping them.

SCENE VII

Albrecht appears, followed by Wilfrid, his faithful squire. The Duke is sad and pale, his dress in disorder[1]; he has almost lost his reason as a result of Giselle's death. He goes slowly towards the cross as if seeking a memory in order to collect his confused thoughts.

Wilfrid entreats Albrecht to accompany him and not to linger near the fatal tomb, which recalls so many sorrows. Albrecht

[1] From the eighteenth until late in the nineteenth century, disordered dress was the traditional stage symbol of a mind deranged.

47

bids him depart. Wilfrid renews his entreaty, but Albrecht orders him so forcefully to leave that the squire is compelled to obey. He goes out determined to make one last effort to induce his master to leave this fatal spot.

SCENE VIII

No sooner is he alone than Albrecht gives vent to his grief. His heart is filled with anguish ; he sheds tears. Suddenly he grows pale, his gaze fixed on a strange being who takes shape before his eyes. He remains stricken with surprise, almost terror, on recognising Giselle, who looks endearingly at him.

SCENE IX

A prey to the most violent delirium, to the most lively anxiety, he still doubts and dare not credit what he sees, for it is not the pretty Giselle whom he adored, but Giselle the Wili, in her new and strange metamorphosis, who remains motionless before him. The Wili seems to invite him with a look. Albrecht, believing himself to be dominated by a charming illusion, goes towards her with slow and cautious steps, like a child desiring to capture a butterfly poised on a flower. But, no sooner does he extend his hand towards Giselle than, quicker than lightning, she darts far away from him, to take flight and soar through the air like a frightened dove, to alight in another quarter, where she throws him loving glances.

This dance, or rather flight, is repeated a second time, to the great despair of Albrecht, who attempts in vain to join the Wili, now and again fleeing before him like a faint wisp of mist. Sometimes, however, she makes him a loving gesture, throws him a flower which she ravishes from its stem, or wafts him a kiss, but, intangible as a cloud, she vanishes just as he believes her within his grasp.

At last he gives up, kneels beside the cross, and places his hands together in an attitude of entreaty. The Wili, as though attracted by this mute sorrow, so charged with love, bounds lightly beside her lover. He touches the Wili, and, swooning with love and happiness, is about to seize her, when, gliding softly between his arms, she vanishes among the roses, while Albrecht brings his arms together to clasp only the cross on the tomb.

Evincing the deepest despair, he rises and is about to leave this abode of sorrow, when he encounters a spectacle so unusual and so fascinating that he is somehow stayed, held fast, and forced to witness the strange scene unfolded to his gaze.

SCENE X

Hidden behind a weeping willow, Albrecht perceives the unfortunate Hilarion, hunted by a whole band of Wilis.

Pale, trembling, and almost dead from fright, the gamekeeper collapses at the foot of a tree and seems to beseech the mercy of his playful enemies. But the Queen of the Wilis, with a touch from her sceptre, forces him to rise and imitate the dance movement which she herself begins to dance about him. Hilarion, impelled by a magic force, dances in spite of himself with the lovely Wili until she surrenders him to one of her companions who, in turn, hands him to another, and so on to the last of all.

Just when the hapless wretch believes his torment ended with his wearied partner, another replaces her with new strength, and, compelled to put forth unimaginable efforts to the ever-quickening rhythm of the music, he ends by staggering and feeling overwhelmed with lassitude and grief.

At last, resolved on a desperate course, he tries to flee; but the Wilis surround him in a great circle which gradually contracts, closes upon him, and becomes changed into a rapid waltz movement, in which a supernatural power forces him to take part. Seized with giddiness, the gamekeeper escapes from the arms of one waltzer only to fall into the power of another. The victim, ever enmeshed in this graceful and deadly web, soon feels his knees give way under him. His eyes close, he can no longer see, yet he continues to dance with a burning frenzy. Then the Queen of the Wilis seizes Hilarion and makes him turn and waltz with her for the last time, until the poor devil, the end link in a chain of waltzers, arrived at the edge of the lake, opens his arms, thinking to clasp a fresh waltzer, and goes tumbling into the abyss. The Wilis, led by their triumphant Queen, begin a joyous bacchanale, when one of their number discovers Albrecht and conducts him, still astounded by what he had just seen, into their magic circle.

SCENE XI

The Wilis seem to congratulate themselves on finding another victim, their cruel band already begins to hover about this new quarry; but, just as Myrtha is about to touch Albrecht with her enchanted wand, Giselle darts forward and restrains the Queen's upraised arm.

Scene XII

" Flee ! " cries Giselle to her beloved, " flee, or thou art a dead man, as dead as Hilarion ! " she adds, pointing to the lake.

Albrecht is momentarily horror-struck at the thought of sharing the gamekeeper's awful fate. Giselle takes advantage of this instant of indecision to seize Albrecht's hand ; impelled by a magic force, together they glide towards the marble cross ; she indicates this sacred symbol as his shield, his only salvation !

The Queen and all the Wilis pursue him to the tomb, but Albrecht, ever protected by Giselle, reaches the cross, which he embraces, and, just as Myrtha is about to touch him with her wand, the enchanted branch breaks in the hand of the Queen, who stands immovable, as do all the Wilis, overcome with surprise and dismay.

Furious at being baulked of their cruel hopes, the Wilis circle about Albrecht, and frequently dart towards him, ever repelled by a power superior to their own. Then the Queen, determined to be revenged upon the one who carried off her victim, stretches out her hand towards Giselle, whose wings immediately open and who begins to dance with the utmost grace and ardour, as if carried away by an involuntary madness.

Albrecht, motionless, watches her, overwhelmed, astounded, at this curious scene, but the Wili's graces and ravishing poses soon attract him against his will, which is what the Queen intended ; he forsakes the holy cross which protects him from death and goes towards Giselle, who pauses from fear and implores him to regain his sacred talisman. But the Queen, touching Giselle anew, forces her to continue her captivating dance. This episode is repeated several times until, giving way at last to the passion which consumes him, Albrecht forsakes the cross and darts towards Giselle. He seizes the enchanted branch, for he would rather die and rejoin the Wili than be parted from her.

Albrecht seems to have wings, he skims the ground and leaps about the Wili, who from time to time endeavours to restrain him. But, carried away by her new nature, Giselle is soon forced to join her lover. They begin a quick, airy, and frenzied dance. They seem to vie with each other in grace and agility. Now and again they pause, to fall into each other's arms ; then the fantastic music lends them new strength and fresh ardour.

The whole band of Wilis accompany the two lovers, surrounding them with sensuous poses.

Albrecht is seized with a deadly weariness. He still struggles, but it is clear that his strength is beginning to be exhausted. Giselle goes to him and pauses for an instant, her eyes filled with tears ; but a sign from the Queen forces her to take flight anew. A few more seconds and Albrecht is about to perish from weariness and exhaustion, when dawn begins to break. The first rays of sunlight illumine the silvered ripples of the lake.

The fantastic and tumultuous round of the Wilis slows down as the night fades away. Giselle seems to be filled with fresh hope on seeing the disappearance of the terrible enchantment which was leading Albrecht to his doom. Subjected to the bright rays of the sun, the whole band of Wilis gradually droop and wilt, and in turn are seen to stagger, expire, and collapse in a clump of flowers, or on the stem which saw them born, like night flowers dying at the approach of day.

During this charming spectacle, Giselle, subject, like her ethereal sisters, to the influence of daylight, slowly frees herself from Albrecht's enfeebled arms. She goes towards her tomb as though impelled by fate. Albrecht, conscious of the doom threatening her, bears Giselle away from the tomb and places her on the mound, amid a tuft of flowers. Then he kneels beside her and kisses Giselle as if to infuse her with his spirit and restore her to life. But Giselle, pointing to the sun, now shining in all its strength, seems to tell him that she must submit to her fate and leave him for evermore.

At this moment loud fanfares echo in the heart of the forest. Albrecht hears them with apprehension and Giselle with a sweet joyfulness.

SCENE XIII

Wilfrid runs in. The faithful squire is ahead of the Prince and Bathilde, accompanied by a numerous suite. He leads them to Albrecht, hoping that their efforts to induce him to leave this vale of sorrow will be more successful than his own.

Everyone stops on seeing him. Albrecht leaps towards his squire to hold him back. Meanwhile, the Wili nears her last moments ; the surrounding flowers and grasses have begun to rise and cover her with their slender stems ; already the graceful phantom is partly concealed.

Albrecht retraces his steps and remains spellbound with surprise and grief on seeing Giselle sink slowly and gradually into this verdant tomb. Then, with one arm she still keeps free, she shows Albrecht the trembling Bathilde, kneeling some paces from him and stretching out her hand to him with a gesture of entreaty.

Giselle seems to tell her lover to bestow his love and fidelity on the sweet young girl; that is her sole wish, her last prayer, from one who can love no more in this world. Then, making him a poignant and eternal gesture of farewell, she vanishes amid the flowering grass which now completely engulfs her.

Albrecht rises heartbroken, but to him the Wili's command seems sacred. He plucks some of the flowers which cover Giselle and lovingly presses them to his heart, next, to his lips, then, weak and staggering, he stretches out his hand to Bathilde and falls into the arms of those surrounding him.

CHAPTER V

ADOLPHE ADAM AND THE MUSIC OF " GISELLE "

THE works of Adolphe Adam are seldom heard in present-day concert programmes, yet he was once among the most popular composers of his time. Nowadays he is principally remembered for his comic opera, *Le Postillon de Lonjumeau*, and the overture to another of his operas, *Si J'étais Roi*, both occasionally performed, and for his music to the ballet, *Giselle*.

Adam was born at Paris on July 24th, 1803. His mother was the daughter of a distinguished physician. His father was a professor of music at the Conservatoire. He was a virtuoso on the piano and also wrote two elementary textbooks regarding that instrument which at one time were used in almost every French school. In addition he composed eleven sonatas for the piano and several other works.

As a boy, Adolphe was very fond of music, but, although he would sit for hours listening to his father playing the piano, he detested the study of music and much preferred improvising melodies of his own. At last his mother tired of his unruliness and sent him to a boarding school, later exchanged for a day school; at both of these he took lessons in music. At the latter institution he made good progress and a friend of his father's also gave him lessons in harmony.

Adolphe, now seventeen, decided to make music his profession, although his father was opposed to the plan. From 1821 he studied at the Conservatoire with Boïeldieu, who continually urged him to concentrate on the composition of vaudevilles and comic operas. Boïeldieu took a great interest in his pupil, to whom he became much attached, and secured for him a commission from a publisher to arrange some selections from popular operas; for this work the young composer received three hundred francs.

Adam, thus unexpectedly enriched, resolved to take a holiday, when he visited Belgium, Holland, Germany, and Switzerland; nor did he neglect the opportunity to note down folk airs that appealed to him. While at Geneva he met the playwright, Eugène Scribe, who told him that he found Switzerland very inspiring for the writing of vaudevilles and comic operas. When Adam replied that he was a composer and had come across many pretty melodies, Scribe promised to see him later in Paris.

On his return the young man did not fail to call on Scribe, who had just completed a short comic opera, for which he invited his visitor to write the music. This production was a decided success and marks Adam's entry into the world of the theatre.

It is beyond the scope of this essay to give a detailed account of all his compositions, for his output attained extraordinary proportions. He wrote forty operas and comic operas, many of them in two or three acts, also many ballets, masses, cantatas, choruses, and songs. But our chief interest is the ballets, of which Adam composed fourteen : *Faust* (Deshayes, 1833), *La Fille du Danube* (F. Taglioni, 1836), *Les Mohicans* (Guerra, 1837), *L'Ecumeur de Mer* (prod. St. Petersburg, 1840), *Les Hamadryades* (prod. Berlin, 1840), *Giselle* (1841), *La Jolie Fille de Gand* (Albert, 1842), *Le Diable à Quatre* (Mazilier, 1845), *The Marble Maiden* (Albert, 1845), *Griselidis, ou les Cinq Sens* (Mazilier, 1848), *La Filleule des Fées* (Perrot, 1849), *Orfa* (Mazilier, 1852) and *Le Corsaire* (Mazilier, 1856).

On November 15th, 1847, Adam founded the Opéra National, to be devoted to the presentation of works by young composers. The initial production and subsequent pieces were so well received that the prosperity of the ambitious venture seemed assured. Then came the revolution of February, 1848. As a result, the new theatre was obliged to close on March 26th and Adam was left with liabilities amounting to 70,000 francs. Manfully he shouldered this crushing burden and by dint of heavy sacrifices and immense labours succeeded by 1852 in paying off the last of his creditors. But the combination of disappointment and overwork undermined even his robust constitution, and a little more than four years later, on May 3rd, 1856, he died in his sleep.

A lithograph (see plate facing p. 53) after a drawing by Cauvin, which is based on a photograph (probably taken in the eighteen-forties since it shows Adam wearing the ribbon of the *Légion d'Honneur* awarded him in 1836), enables us to visualise the composer who, according to a contemporary, was short and stocky. He has a broad-browed, square-shaped head, plump features, straight nose, and thick lips half hidden beneath a full moustache and close-cropped, straggling beard. The eyes, screened by gold-rimmed spectacles, have a malicious twinkle in them. But the face as a whole, with its alert and shrewd expression, suggests a man of business, a physician, or a technical consultant rather than a votary of the arts.

Adam was endowed with a tireless energy, for almost every day was wholly taken up with his innumerable activities—rehearsals, visits, financial discussions, attendance at the Institut or the Conservatoire, calls on newspaper editors, appointments with music publishers, and attendances at concerts and theatres. Indeed, he had sometimes to contrive to be present at two first nights on the same evening. In addition, his home was always " open house " to his friends.

But after supper he would go into his little salon, lift up his coat-tails, and warm his back before the fire. After a little while he would turn to his friends and remark, " Now, I must drive you away ! " Then he would begin to compose. " It is so nice to work in the evening," he used to say, " one has the whole night before one ; in the daytime one is so disturbed."

Mention has already been made of Adam's extraordinary capacity for work, to which he united an unusual facility in the devising of light and tuneful melodies. He had only to open his piano and place his fingers on the keyboard when themes came to mind almost as quickly as he could play them. He developed these ideas in an elegant harmonisation and by means of a colourful orchestration.

As an example of his speed, Adam himself tells us that he wrote *Le Châlet*, an opera in one act, in a fortnight ; and *Le Toréador*, a comic opera in two acts, in eight days. He was frequently criticised for his speed of composition. But Adam rightly argued that a work is not necessarily important because it has taken a long time to achieve, and asserted that his most successful works were those which had been composed in a few days. The explanation of his tireless activity is that Adam, like Balzac, was obsessed with a craving to produce, a craving which increased even when he was in the very throes of creation.

The music for *Giselle* was also composed quickly. Gautier suggests that the score was completed in less than a week. In his unpublished *Mémoires*[1] Adam records in one place that *Giselle* took eight days, and, in another, three weeks.[2] *Giselle* is conceived in the *cantilena* style made popular by the operas

[1] Pougin (Arthur), *Op. cit.*, p. 161.
[2] Quoted Pougin (Arthur), *Op. cit.*, see p. 96 (footnote).

of Bellini and Donizetti; it abounds in flowing melodies and simple dance rhythms.

By no stretch of imagination can the score of *Giselle* be called great music, but it cannot be denied that it is admirably suited to its purpose. It is danceable, and it has colour and mood attuned to the various dramatic situations. Again, since ballet is a composite art, it is not altogether fair to consider music apart from the dancing with which it is intended it shall be fused, for only in actual performance can the worth of a musical score—as ballet music—be assessed at its full value.

A remarkable feature of *Giselle* is Adam's use of *Leitmotiv*, that is, the association of a particular melodic theme or phrase with a certain character or incident. For instance, Hilarion's theme, a quotation of the Fate theme from Beethoven's *Fifth Symphony*, which marks Hilarion's every entrance; the theme for the flower test of fidelity, and the theme for the love scene between Giselle and Loys, both of which recur during the scene of madness; the Wilis's theme, which is first heard when Giselle's mother warns her daughter of the dangers of dancing to excess, is repeated during the scene of madness, and again used to announce the entry of the Wilis; and, finally, the huntsmen's theme, which is heard twice during the first act.

The music of *Giselle* aroused considerable interest among the professional critics and in this connection it is of interest to quote, as an indication of contemporary opinion, the long analysis by Escudier in *La France Musicale* (July 4th, 1841).

"To devise original music for a theme so perfectly handled by MM. de Saint-Georges and Théophile Gautier, all M. Adolphe Adam's imagination and verve were needed. This composer, who has already given us *La Fille du Danube*, has this time accomplished a real feat. His ballet is particularly noteworthy for its elegance, for the freshness and variety of its melodies, for its bold and novel harmonic combinations, for a zest which grips you from the very outset and is maintained to the end.

"As a general rule, ballet music does not carry much weight; among the innumerable ballets presented at the Opera, it is difficult to mention more than three in which the composer revealed some signs of imagination. They are *La Somnambule*, *La Sylphide*, and *La Fille du Danube*. Méhul and Cherubini have also written ballet music in their day, but then it was little more than a matter of arrangement, the symphonies of Hadyn and Mozart being the common source from which the composers drew their dance themes.

" The music of *Giselle* is wholly original. As regards borrow-ings,[1] there are no more than eight bars from a romance by Mlle. Puget and three bars of the huntsmen's chorus from *Euryanthé*,[2] which are woven with the greatest skill into the texture of the piece of which they form the opening.

" M. Adam's score has been so generally acclaimed that we feel it incumbent on us to make an analysis of a work which is as meritorious as many an opera that has achieved undoubted success.

" At the rise of the curtain we find a charming introduction, where the orchestration is quite in Cherubini's manner ; this introduction has perhaps one defect, that of not being long enough. The first scene between Giselle and Loys includes some very attractive numbers, then comes a ravishing waltz, where the theme is quite in the German style, and which may well become as popular as the most beautiful of Strauss's[3] waltzes. This waltz is interrupted by the entrance of Giselle's mother, who depicts to her daughter the danger of dancing to excess, and her own dread of seeing her one day changed into a Wili. The music of this scene contains some quite new modulations. This piece is followed by hunting-calls. Here the use of brass is very happy and seldom have we heard this type of instrument written for in so favourable a compass, obtaining power and sonority without any stridency. The little *andante* movement to which takes place the scene between Giselle and the *fiancée* of Loys, is delightful in its artlessness and style. *The divertissement* begins with a vine-gatherers' march in a bold and original rhythm. The progression of a third, G to B flat, followed always by the chord of D major, produces a very unusual effect. The *pas de deux* between Giselle and Loys ends with a *mouve-ment louré*[4] which is most pleasing. The Galop which concludes

[1] In addition to the few bars noted by Escudier, the original score of the first act contained two interpolated compositions by Fr. Burgmüller—a waltz entitled " Souvenir de Ratisbonne " and a suite of dances which used to be performed by Giselle's friends and their two leaders. I do not know, however, why or on whose authority these numbers were introduced. When the ballet proved to be a success, Burgmüller's publisher, Colombier, brought out a new edition of the waltz, with the sub-title " dansée par Mlle. Nathalie FitzJames et Mabille dans Giselle."

[2] Opera by Carl von Weber, first performed Vienna, 1823.

[3] Johann Strauss (Johann I, 1804–48). the founder of the famous Viennese family of dance composers. It is the works of his youngest son (Johann II, 1825–99), the composer of such popular melodies as the *Blue Danube*, which are best known to-day.

[4] A movement which imitates the music of the bagpipe. *Loure* was the name given to a bagpipe used by Normandy peasants ; and *Loure* was also the name of a rustic dance once accompanied by the bagpipes.

the *divertissement* is of less value than the numbers which preceded it, but the rhythm is so inspiring that it is all a galop
should be. The finale of the first act, which consists of the
Mad Scene, forms in all its phases a complete work, and we
doubt if there is a better finale in the whole of the operas of
the composer of *Le Châlet*, *Le Postillon*, and *La Reine d'un
Jour*.

"But whatever pleasure was afforded by the music of the first
act, it was insignificant to what the composer had kept back
for the second. It would be too difficult to analyse each
number in that act, however, we must mention the very novel
orchestral effect which accompanies the appearance of the
Queen of the Wilis; over arpeggi on the harp, four muted
first violins play in their highest register a four-part melody
for strings, whose effect is truly magical. One really does feel
suddenly transported to the realm of fairyland. This combination is entirely new and the effect excellent. Then, in succession
to this, there are several dance airs whose rhythm is always
varied, without the fantastic colouring ceasing for a moment
to dominate these ethereal melodies. Musically, this is the most
remarkable part of the ballet. It is the first time we have seen
the fantastic treated with due regard to grace and charm, and
perhaps it never will be more happily achieved. Giselle's final
dance is accompanied by a viola solo which is admirably played
by M. Urhan. Nothing could be sweeter or more melancholy
than the quality of that instrument so rarely employed melodi-
cally. The phrase to which Giselle vanishes amid the flowers,
which phrase is sustained solely by the flute and harps, is full
of tragic beauty. This phrase affords a lovely conclusion to
this scene, which may well achieve both a popular and fashionable success."

As we listen to-day to these haunting melodies composed
over a century ago, we quickly become conscious of their
intense nostalgic quality, not unlike the emotion produced by
the opening of a Victorian *Keepsake*, between whose pages lies
an admirably preserved Valentine—in all the glory of its intricate
paper lace and symbolic floral designs—which whispers of
a leisured age now for ever past. For a brief space the air
seems faintly perfumed with the fragrance of parma violet
and gardenia. The music of *Giselle* still exerts its magic. It
is no less potent than the Wilis in its power to captivate and
enchant those members of the audience willing to surrender
to its mood.

CHAPTER VI

SOME SETTINGS FOR "GISELLE"

THE original scenery for *Giselle* was designed by Pierre Luc Charles Ciceri (1782–1868), who was chief designer of settings to the Paris Opera from 1815 to 1847 and associated with over 300 productions. He was noted for his scenic representations of moonlit buildings and landscapes such as the abbey interior in Meyerbeer's opera, *Robert le Diable,* and the famous glade in *La Sylphide,* ever associated with Marie Taglioni. Such scenes, like his setting for the second act of *Giselle,* were the embodiment of that strange blend of the material and immaterial, that paradoxical compound of two diametrically opposed elements—picturesque spectacle and the sphere of fantastic visions—known as romanticism.

The synopsis of *Giselle* is not very communicative as to the period, time, or place of the ballet. But although there is no mention of period, since the ballet opens with the festival of grape-gathering, the season of autumn is clearly indicated. As to place, we are told that the action passes in Germany, "on the borders of Thuringia"—that is, in central Germany. But, in his notice of the first performance of the ballet, Gautier is more informative. "The action," he says, "takes place in a vague country, in Silesia, in Thuringia, even in one of the Bohemian sea-ports that Shakespeare loved : it suffices for it to be on the other side of the Rhine, in some mysterious corner of Germany."[1]

I have not seen Ciceri's original designs for the settings of *Giselle,* and since realisation sometimes diverges from conception, I shall have recourse to the contemporary sketches of the ballet reproduced in a volume entitled *Les Beautés de l'Opéra,* published at Paris in 1844, which includes a description of the ballet by Gautier himself. The wood engraving at the head of the essay on *Giselle* gives us a very clear idea of what the setting for the first act was like. It shows two thatched cottages, one on either side of the stage ; that of Giselle is on the spectator's left ; that of Loys on his right. Both cottages are seen from the frontal aspect and each is shaded by the

[1] *Op. cit.,* Vol. II, p. 134.

spreading branches of an ancient tree which grows beside it. In front of Loys's cottage there is a rustic bench. A winding road passes between the two dwellings to be lost among the vine-covered slopes in the background. In the far distance, dominating the slopes, rises a rocky height crowned with a castle.

This scene continued to be used throughout the cycle of performances given at the Opera between 1841 and 1853, for Gautier, reviewing one of the last performances, comments, " *Giselle* was revived with Mlle. Regina Forli for interpreter. The settings of the ballet begin wretchedly to expose the canvas ; the sky needs sweeping, the yellow leaves of the vines fall and whirl like the golden specks in Dantzic brandy . . . Giselle's cottage has no more than three or four straws on its roof, and what straw ! as Janin would say."[1] This scene, with slight alterations in the size and style of the cottages, type of tree, and castle-crowned rock, has remained constant in its essentials, and, speaking broadly, has served as pattern for all other settings for the opening scene of this ballet.

The setting for the second act is also depicted in *Les Beautés de l'Opéra*, as well as suggested in various contemporary lithographs of Grisi in this scene. It presents a glade in a dense forest. To left and right is an avenue of giant trees whose leafy branches intertwine to form a series of natural arches. Through the arches can be seen in the distance the placid surface of a dark pool, faintly gleaming in the light shed by the rising moon. In the left foreground is a cross, inscribed Giselle, and a mound, half hidden beneath clusters of rushes and wild flowers, which marks her grave. The glade is carpeted with a thick undergrowth. While the scene is attractive in its mystery and natural beauty, it arouses a sense of apprehension as to what dangers may lurk amid its leafy recesses.

This setting was carried out in the realistic style then in vogue, and the stage must have been rather crowded for, in connection with his scheme, the designer used some 200 bullrushes and 120 branches of flowers with their leaves. An atmosphere at once sinister and mysterious was produced by lowering the gas jets of the footlights and those of the boxed jets suspended from the flies. This effect of semi-obscurity served to emphasise the phantom-like quality of the white-clad Wilis flitting among the reeds. The effect of moonlight was achieved by the simple means of cutting a circular hole in the backcloth and covering

[1] *La Presse*, April 25th, 1853.

it with transparent material, then placing a strong light immediately behind it. From time to time the light was varied to suggest the passing of clouds by revolving vari-shaped discs behind the aperture.

The literary parents of *Giselle* set great store by the effect of the pool and wished it to be formed from an arrangement of mirrors, a stage illusion often used in London theatres and introduced to Paris by the French stage designer, Chéret. The management, however, declined the effect on the ground of expense.

It is of interest to record that when *Giselle* was revived at the Opera in 1863 for the Paris *début* of the Russian *ballerina*, Martha Muravieva, the then director, Emile Perrin, not only commissioned new settings and costumes, but also provided the long-coveted pool, formed by two large mirrors placed some distance apart at the rear of the stage and parallel to the footlights. The mirrors were set at a slight angle so that the audience could see the surrounding trees reflected in what they imagined to be the surface of the pool. Again, a Wili passing between the two mirrors from one side of the stage to the other was reflected in the mirror furthest from the stage, and so suggested a phantom-like figure winging its way over the pool.

Here is Gautier's prose picture of this same scene, again taken from his notice of the *première*. " The stage represents a forest on the banks of a pool; you see tall pale trees, whose roots spring from the grass and the rushes; the water-lily spreads its broad leaves on the surface of the placid water, which the moon silvers here and there with a trail of white spangles. Reeds with their brown velvet sheaths shiver and palpitate beneath the intermittent night breeze. The flowers open languorously and exhale a giddy perfume like those broad flowers of Java which madden whoever inhales their scent. I cannot say what burning and sensuous atmosphere flows about this humid and leafy obscurity. At the foot of a willow, asleep and concealed beneath the flowers, lies poor Giselle. From the marble cross which indicates her grave is suspended, still quite fresh, the garland of vine branches with which she had been crowned at the vintage festival."[1]

And here is another description by Gautier of the same scene, taken from his essay in *Les Beautés de l'Opéra* (1844), and presumably written at a later date. It will be noticed that

[1] *Op. cit.*, Vol. II, p. 138.

here the *mysterious* quality of the scene is stressed, while, in the first account, the accent is on the *sensuous* atmosphere of the glen. This difference may be due to some change in the lighting.

" One of those mysterious forests such as are found in Sadeler's engravings. Huge trees with strangely twisted trunks interlace their inextricable branches, while their gnarled roots, like so many thirsty snakes, bury themselves in the black and stagnant water, on which the giant leaves of water-lilies viscously unfold ; tall grasses and weeds mingle with the rushes of the pool, whose velvet plumes shiver in the night air.

" A bluish mist fills the gaps between the trees, causing them to assume fantastic shapes, and changing them into spectral beings. Is not the silvery shaft of that aspen alarmingly like the pale shroud of a ghost ? And does not the transparent pallor of the sad and sweet opal countenance of the rising moon, showing through the gaps in the leaves, suggest some young German girl dead from consumption while reading the works of Novalis ? The whole of the forest seems full of sighs and tears. Is it really the dew or the rain that has attached that pearl to the tip of that blade of grass ? Is it really the wind which sobs as it passes through the reeds ? Why is the velvet sward pressed down in certain places ? No human foot has trod this way, and it is not from this side that herds of deer go down to slake their thirst at the waters of the pool. This faint sweetish aroma does not come from wild flowers ; neither the bell-flower nor the forget-me-not have such a perfume. You are about to solve this mystery."

The main features of this scene then are : (*a*) a sensuous and humid atmosphere, (*b*) a tree-bordered glade almost tropical in its dense vegetation, (*c*) a moonlit pool, (*d*) a single tomb half hidden beneath tufts of grasses and headed with a marble cross.

I have described this second scene in some detail because, unlike that for the first act, it has become far removed from its first conception. Take, for instance, the setting designed by Alexandre Benois for Diaghilev's Russian Ballet season at Paris in 1910. This scene depicts a forest glade of ancient trees with their spreading branches interlocked to form a succession of natural arches, but the branches are bare of foliage. In the distance gleams not the all important pool, but the outline of a church, white in the rays of the moon. In the foreground is a stone cross.

But the whole atmosphere is bleak and wintry and, so far from being inviting and sensuous, nothing could be more awe-inspiring than the sight of those gaunt trees whose branches resemble bony fingers groping towards the sky. It is the kind of place which a wayfarer would instinctively avoid.

Most other designs for this scene, ranging over various settings of the last thirty years, lack some or all of the chief features of the original setting. Yet the successful presentation of this hint of the world of the supernatural demands the preservation of those characteristics which I have grouped under four heads.

The majority of recent productions either omit the pool or stress it to the exclusion of other important details. Simplification is an admirable quality so long as it does not banish atmosphere. On the other hand, there is also a tendency to be over-fanciful. William Chappell, for instance, the designer of more than one setting for the Sadler's Wells Ballet, introduces numerous clumps of lilies and a garlanded classical urn. In another setting for the same scene he depicts a multitude of gravestones which suggest that Giselle's tomb is situated near a necropolis. Such inventions introduce a note of sophistication which is alien to the simple touching story of this rustic tragedy.

Giselle is a period piece in which theme, setting, music, and choreography all belong to the romantic era. Any attempt to transplant it into another period, to modernise it, to smarten it up with bright patches of colour typical of sets for present-day revues, is to invite disaster. The *patina* of a hundred years is not easily to be removed.

CHAPTER VII

SOME COSTUMES FOR "GISELLE"

THE synopsis of *Giselle*, as already stated, is silent as to the period of the ballet. The designer of the costumes, Paul Lormier, must, however, have received some direction on this important matter, probably from Gautier, unless the choice of period was influenced to some extent by the possibility of fitting out the *corps de ballet* and supers with portions of costumes borrowed from the Opera's extensive wardrobe. It is said that the principal sources of supply were the costumes of two operas —Rossini's *Guillaume Tell* (1829) and Berlioz's *Benvenuto Cellini* (1838)—and Mazilier's ballet, *Le Diable Amoureux* (1840), all of which were set in the Renaissance period. This was a recognised practice and, as we know from the matter of the mirrors, Léon Pillet was a firm believer in economy. The period of the ballet may therefore be defined broadly as the middle ages, for the costumes range from the fourteenth to the sixteenth centuries.

Lormier was attached to the Opera as a costume designer from 1831. He became *Chef de l'Habillement* in 1855, which post he retained until 1887. Apart from occasional flights of fancy, he was a serious student of historic costume and took great pains to ensure accuracy of detail. Lormier's costume designs for the characters of *Giselle*, with his marginal notes regarding the materials to be used, are still preserved in the Bibliothèque de l'Opéra. It will be of interest to quote some of these details in order that the reader may form some idea of the appearance originally presented by the various characters.

ACT ONE

Hilarion. Tawny coloured fur cap; gold braided jerkin of padded green cloth; leather belt with hunting knife and hunting-horn; green woollen hose; laced boots with turned down tops.

Albrecht. Black cloth barret[1]; jerkin of purple cloth with violet sleeves; grey silk hose; black shoes.

Wilfrid. Black velvet barret with a peacock's feather; jerkin of buff cloth with purple bands and sky-blue sleeves; leather belt with dagger; sky-blue hose; grey boots.

Giselle. Blue wimple; bodice of light brown velvet; skirt of buttercup yellow; narrow white apron. If the original designs (there are two versions for this costume) be compared with the engraving by Robinson after the painting of Grisi by A. E. Chalon (see plate facing this page), it is clear that the bodice must have been considerably modified during realisation. It will be noticed that the bodice is " off the shoulders " and that the original wide sleeves are close fitting and scarcely extend beyond the biceps. Again, the practical apron of the original conception becomes a coquettish symbol reminiscent of that worn by a stage parlourmaid.

Prince of Courland. Black velvet barret; gold braided jerkin of green velvet with white sleeves; grey woollen hose; laced boots.

Bathilde. Black velvet barret braided with gold and adorned with white plumes; riding habit of green velvet with white sleeves.

Peasant Girls. Black velvet headdress; black bodice over white blouse; skirt of sky blue, violet, pink, buff, or brown; white apron; white stockings; puce coloured shoes.

Peasant Youths. Cloth barret of yellow, blue, sky blue, red, violet, or purple; cloth jerkin of grey, blue, buff, black, brown, or grey; leather belt; blue, brown, or red socks; black shoes.

Ladies in Hunting Dress. Velvet barret of red, violet, or black, with white plumes; riding habit and cape in buff, red, violet, light green, or dark green.

Noblemen in Hunting Dress. Grey felt hat; emerald green jerkin puffed at the elbow; leather belt with dagger; green hose; leather boots. A hunting horn, suspended by a red cord, is slung from the left shoulder.

---

[1] Flat cap similar to a tam-o'-shanter, a form of headgear much favoured during the fifteenth century.

ACT TWO

Myrtha. Garland of verbena and white flowers, with a silver star set above the centre of the forehead ; white bodice with blue and silver wings below the shoulders ; white skirt decorated with four white flowers ; flesh-coloured tights ; ballet shoes.

Wilis. The Bibliothèque de l'Opéra does not contain a design by Lormier for a Wili, but there is a drawing by an anonymous artist, clearly not Lormier. Low-necked white dress reaching to the top of the calf, the top of the bodice edged with green ribbon, with a silver girdle at the waist ; pair of small transparent wings attached to the shoulders. The skirt is split half-way down the right thigh to the hem, the opening being caught by three little bunches of verbena[1] flowers. Three short petticoats are worn beneath the skirt, but the artist, in a marginal note, stresses the necessity for the costume to be as diaphanous as possible. The costume would seem to have been more like a classic *peplum* drawn in at the waist.

Albrecht. Black velvet barret with a peacock's feather ; jerkin of primrose velvet embroidered in gold ; yellow satin sleeves slashed with white and yellow ; black velvet belt ; white silk hose ; black shoes.

Lormier's costumes remained in use at the Opera until 1853, when the ballet was withdrawn from performance until 1863, the date at which *Giselle* was revived for the Paris *début* of the Russian *ballerina*, Martha Muravieva, and provided with new costumes by Lormier's assistant, Alfred Albert, of whose work I reproduce four examples as shown in contemporary photographs (see plates facing pages 36 and 37).

The costumes for Hilarion and the Prince of Courland are appropriate and show a careful regard for period. It is interesting also to note that Hilarion looks like a sturdy gamekeeper and not an effeminate youth, and that the Prince has an air of dignified authority. Hilarion has the short tufted beard which in productions of later years becomes fuller and longer.

---

[1] Verbena or vervain is a plant with small blue, white, or purple flowers. It was once known as " holy herb " owing to its use in sacrificial rites.

Muravieva's costumes conform to the style of ballet dress at this period (1863). The costume for the first act is the typical peasant's dress, ballet style, with its velvet bodice and full skirt decorated near the hem with bands of silk or velvet ribbon. This is the type of costume—allowing for modern simplification of cut and design—usually worn nowadays, the bodice is generally a dark blue velvet, the skirt a pale blue, the apron white. The Russian *ballerina*, Olga Spessivtzeva, made an innovation by wearing a very short skirt for the first act (see plate facing page 103). It may be of interest to mention that her costume consisted of pale pink tights, blue shoes, white lace skirt with a trailer of tiny blue flowers decorating two of the tiers, and sapphire blue satin bodice ornamented with small brass buttons ; her hair was bound with a blue ribbon into which was twisted a tiny posy of cowslips. The costume for the second act is in the style of the pure classical ballet : close fitting bodice and bell-shaped skirt.

The white ballet skirt has long remained the traditional costume for the Wilis, and, despite attempts to vary it by adding strings of leaves and exotic headdresses, or by making the Wilis resemble fashionable bridesmaids, it is not easy to improve upon. Consider, for instance, the charming dress worn by Spessivtzeva (see plate facing page 128), made of *tulle*, not tarlatan ; while both tights and shoes were white. There is, however, another variation from type which must be mentioned. Pavlova, who during her appearance as Giselle at the Maryinsky Theatre, St. Petersburg, always wore the traditional ballet skirt for the second act, used a quite different costume when she had a company of her own. She devised a white muslin robe in the classical style, which had the appearance of a shroud ; the other Wilis wore a similar costume coloured grey-green and palest blue. To the best of my belief, this is the only instance of such a costume being used in this connection.

Albert's costumes remained in use until 1868, by which date *Giselle* had been performed at the Opera 143 times. The ballet then suffered from neglect until 1924 when the then director of the Opera, Jacques Rouché, decided to present Spessivtzeva in the famous ballet. The costumes, like the settings, for this production were designed by Alexandre Benois. These, as will be seen from the examples facing page 68, are in accordance with tradition, but interpreted in a more refined and artistic manner.

This, of course, was not the first time Benois had designed costumes for this ballet. He was responsible for those used in the production of *Giselle* at Paris in 1910 by Diaghilev's Ballet Russe, with Karsavina and Nijinsky as Giselle and Albrecht. Benois, in his *Reminiscences* [1], describes some of the difficulties he encountered. He wished to design costumes in the style and spirit of those used in the original production, believing that the stressing of certain period oddities of dress might afford piquancy to the production. But he finally decided to abandon this plan, fearing he might be accused of lack of invention.

One of the most charming of Benois' costumes is that for Albrecht in the first act: a short-sleeved jerkin of brown cloth over a white shirt, grey hose and brown shoes. This has always seemed to me an ideal costume and far superior to the present close-fitting doublet which ends at the navel to meet the top of the tights, affording a hard and uncouth appearance to the wearer. After all, Albrecht has merely donned the dress of a peasant youth; there is no need for him to resemble a circus acrobat. This suggestion is heightened when the cuffs and collars are frequently devoid of a white edging of shirt; and all suggestion of period is ruined by the determined refusal of some dancers to wear an appropriate wig and content themselves with their own closely cropped hair.

Benois also devised an admirable costume for Albrecht in the second act. It originally consisted of a dark jerkin and trunks, lightly slashed, white hose and black shoes, and Nijinsky, for whom the costume was designed, wore the dress with grace and distinction. It must be admitted, however, that the length of the trunks needs to be nicely adjusted to suit the dancer's legs, or the result may detract from his appearance.

But, as a general rule, Albrecht's costume for the second act leaves much to be desired. Albrecht, heartbroken and distracted with grief, has come to pay his last respects to the grave of his beloved Giselle. Surely, then, there is no need for him to appear in a deep purple doublet, mauve tights of a vivid hue, and a black cloak lined with the same violent mauve. Nor on the other hand, is it quite fitting for the Duke to appear in a richer version of the acrobat's costume sometimes worn in act one. There is still another type in which Albrecht wears an absurdly elaborate costume, slashed and decorated

---

[1] *Reminiscences of the Russian Ballet,* 1941.

to such excess that the wearer resembles one of Henri ⁷ mignons.

It should not be difficult to devise a costume of a sobᵤ sombre richness, for instance, a dark velvet costume in the Hamlet manner, relieved with a few slashes, the sleeves and collar edged with white so that the dancer's figure is not lost against the dark background. Again, he should be provided with a cloak which a nobleman might reasonably be expected to don when visiting a lonely wood at midnight and not a garment more suited to a fancy dress ball. However, as Gautier has observed in one of his charming essays, one must not expect precise logic in a ballet. Granted, yet, for the writer at least the rare elegiac quality of the beautiful second act is frequently ruined by deficiencies and vulgarities in the design of certain costumes.

CHAPTER VIII

THE ORIGINAL INTERPRETERS OF THE CHIEF RÔLES IN "GISELLE"

THE rôles of Giselle, Myrtha, and Bathilde were create d, as we know, by Carlotta Grisi, Adèle Dumilâtre, and Mlle. Forster, called by Gautier "the three Graces of the Opera."

Carlotta Grisi was born on June 28th, 1819, at Visinida, a little village in Upper Istria. She was cousin to the *prima donna*, Giulia Grisi. Carlotta early revealed an unusual aptitude for dancing, and her parents decided that she should study dancing at the School of Ballet attached to the Scala Theatre, Milan, where she had a Frenchman, M. Guillet, for teacher. There she made such rapid progress that she was appointed leader of a group of child dancers. Her success was immediate and she became known as "the little Héberlé," that being the name of the *première danseuse* at the Scala at this period. Indeed, Grisi's success was almost her downfall, for the public wanted her to dance more and more ; as a consequence her health gave way under the strain and she was obliged to renounce the Dance, fortunately, only for a time.

But, while Carlotta was primarily a dancer, she followed in the family tradition by being blessed with a voice in addition. The celebrated Pasta, having heard her singing one night behind the scenes, pressed her to develop her voice and promised her a wonderful future. She even offered to take her to London, where she herself was to sing, but Carlotta wished only to dance.

Presently her health improved and she secured an engagement with the impresario, Laneri, who sent her on a tour of the principal Italian towns, at each of which she made a triumphant success. It was in 1836, while dancing at Naples, that she made the acquaintance of Jules Perrot, who immediately recognised her rare qualities. Having lacked a teacher for so long, she eagerly placed herself under his guidance and later agreed to become his partner both on the stage and in private life.

Grisi made her first appearance with Perrot on April 12th

of the same year at the King's Theatre, London, in the ballet, *Le Rossignol*, where she danced with him in a *pas de deux*. The critic of *The Times* recorded his impression of Grisi thus : " Her style is peculiar, a mixture of the impassioned, the graceful, and the powerful, blended with much art, and always effective. Her revolving motion in bounding across the stage was wonderful for its flexibility, and exciting from its novelty. Her figure is good, and if it were safe to say from a distant view, we should say she is a very pretty woman. . . . Her reception and the applause at the end of the *pas de deux* with Perrot were enthusiastic."

The first important part to be created by Grisi was that of the title-rôle in *Giselle*. Gautier acclaimed her interpretation as " the greatest choreographic triumph since *La Sylphide*." From this it may be gathered that *Giselle* was to Grisi what *La Sylphide* was to Taglioni and *Le Diable Boiteux* to Fanny Elssler. Gautier then sums up her achievement : " Carlotta danced with a perfection, lightness, boldness, and a chaste and refined seductiveness, which place her in the front rank, between Elssler and Taglioni ; as for pantomime, she exceeded all expectations ; not a single conventional gesture, not one false moment ; she was nature and artlessness personified."[1]

The critic of the *Moniteur des Théâtres* is even more enthusiastic, and contributes an interesting picture of Grisi " in action." " What a charming dancer," he continues, " and how she dances. . . . Imagine then that, from one end of *Giselle* to the other, she is perpetually *en l'air* or *sur les pointes*. In the first act she runs, flies, bounds over the stage like an amorous gazelle ; so much so that the peace of the tomb does not seem too deep for so many races and such expenditure of effort. And yet this is nothing compared with what the second act has in store for her. There, not only must she dance again as just now, but in addition she must be a thousand times more ethereal and intangible, so to speak, because she is a shade. She has no ground to stand upon, no point of support. She cleaves the air like a swallow, perches on the rushes, and leans from the tree-tops, which is the literal truth, to cast flowers to her lover. Do you remember the Sylphide's swift and sudden appearances ? . . . Giselle is a sylphide who has not a single moment's rest."

The first result of Grisi's success was that Pillet offered her an immediate contract as *première danseuse*, which position she

---

[1] *Op. cit.*, Vol. II, p. 142.

retained under his successors, Duponchel and Nestor Roqueplan, until 1849. At the Opera she created the principal rôles of Beatrix in *La Jolie Fille de Gand* (1842), the Peri in *La Péri* (1843), Mazourka in *Le Diable à Quatre* (1845), Paquita in *Paquita*, Griseldis in *Griseldis ou le Cinq Sens* (1848), and Ysaure in *La Filleule des Fées* (1849).

What was Grisi like ? Here is a charming portrait by Gautier. " Carlotta, despite her Italian origin and name, is fair, or at least light chestnut; she has blue eyes of an unusual limpidity and softness. Her mouth is small, dainty, childlike and nearly always tending to a fresh, natural smile, very different from that stereotyped grin usually seen on the lips of actresses. Her complexion is of the rarest delicacy and freshness ; she reminds one of a tea-rose about to flower. She has a well set-up body which, although slender and light, has nothing of that attenuated anatomy which so often makes dancers resemble race-horses in training—all bone and muscle. With her, there is never any sense of weariness or hard work, she is happy to dance for sheer love of it, like a young girl at her first ball, and, however difficult the thing she has to do, she does it as though it were the merest trifle, which is as it should be ; because in the arts nothing is so disagreeable as a difficulty obviously overcome."[1]

Lest this picture might be thought over-flattering, here is a miniature study by the English musical critic, Henry Chorley, writing of her appearance in *Giselle* at Her Majesty's Theatre, London. " She had not the dancer's face, with its set smile put on to disguise breathless distress and fatigue—but she looked shy, and young, and delicate and fresh—there was something of the briar-rose in her beauty."[2]

During her holidays she appeared annually at Her Majesty's Theatre, London, from 1842 to 1850, where, apart from reviving her Paris successes, she created the rôle of Esmeralda in *La Esmeralda* (1844) ; danced in the *Pas de Quatre* in company with Marie Taglioni, Lucile Grahn, and Fanny Cerito ; created the rôle of Fire in *Les Eléments* (1847) ; of Summer in *Les Quatre Saisons* (1848) ; of Electra in *Electra* (1849) ; and of the Sprite in *Les Metamorphoses* (1850).

Grisi made her London *début* in *Giselle* on March 12th, 1842, at Her Majesty's Theatre. That ballet, preceded by Donizetti's opera, *Gemma de Vergy*, was chosen to open the London opera season. The cast included Louise Fleury (*Myrtha*), Jules Perrot

---

[1] *Galerie des Artistes Dramatiques de Paris*, 1841.
[2] *Thirty Years' Musical Recollections*, 2 Vols., 1862.

(*Albrecht*), presumably his first appearance in that rôle, and Eugène Coulon (*Hilarion*). That Grisi repeated her Paris triumph is clear from the long notice devoted to the ballet by *The Times*, [1] from which I quote the following :

" Carlotta Grisi is the heroine, and very beautifully does she give the character of Giselle. Her dancing is marked by a graceful ease, by a complete ' naturalness ' ; the *tours de force* which she executes are completely without effort, without the slightest appearance of exertion. She may be said to belong rather to the school of Taglioni than to that of Cerito. The conception of the character of Giselle is refined. Her first appearance as she bounded from her cottage on the stage was completely illustrative of that joyous carelessness which is supposed to be the first state of the Silesian maiden. Exceedingly well devised was the dance previous to the death of Giselle. The fling of the arms, the joyless movement was supernatural ; it was an anticipation of the ghostly scene of the second act. In this scene there was one touch particularly fine—it was the sudden paroxysm of unearthly joy which took possession of the hitherto quiet spectre, when first made a Wili, by the imposition of a crown on her head. One rapid whirl marked the transition from the inhabitant of the grave to the reckless sprite. An easy voluptuousness is often a pleasing characteristic of Carlotta Grisi's dancing ; the indolent fall into the arms of Perrot, without an effort to sustain herself, was one of her happiest achievements."

Grisi also appeared at Brussels (1847), Berlin (1849), and finally at St. Petersburg, where, on October 8th, 1850, she made her *début* in *Giselle*. Her position was a difficult one, because she had to follow Taglioni and Elssler, both of whom had firmly endeared themselves to the Russian public, and she was nine years older than when she had created that famous rôle. The Russian critics paid tribute to her technique and praised highly the rounded grace of her movements and the brilliancy of her *pointe* work. But they thought she lacked the personality that distinguished Taglioni and Elssler, and seemed more interested in dancing as dancing and not as a means of expressing the theme of the ballet.

Grisi remained three years in the Russian capital, where Perrot, then *maître de ballet* to the Imperial Theatres, produced for her two new ballets, *La Guerre des Femmes ou les Amazones du Neuvième Siecle* (1852) and *Gazelda ou les Tziganes* (1853). She

[1] March 14th.

stage in 1854 and enjoyed a long and happy life in retire-
She died near Geneva on May 22nd, 1899.

*   *   *   *

he first Myrtha was Adèle Dumilâtre (*circa* 1821–1906), one
he two sisters Dumilâtre, Adèle and Sophie, who were both
dancers at the Opera. Their father was a former member of
the Opera orchestra. Both sisters were capable artistes, but
while Adèle was the more beautiful, Sophie was the better
dancer.

Here is Gautier's description of the former's entrance in
Giselle. "The reeds part and first we see a tiny twinkling star,
next a chaplet of flowers, then two startled blue eyes set in an
alabaster oval, and last of all, the whole of that beautiful, slender,
chaste, and graceful form known as Adèle Dumilâtre."[1]

Adam, in his letter[2] to Saint-Georges, confirms the poet's
impression. "La Dumilâtre, despite her coldness, deserved
the success she obtained by the precise and mythological character
of her poses, this word will perhaps seem a little high-flown
to you ; but I cannot find another to express the noble and cold
style of dancing which would suit Minerva in a merry mood.
And, in that respect, Mlle. Dumilâtre seems to me greatly to
resemble that Goddess."

*   *

*

Mlle. Forster, the original Bathilde, would seem to have been
blue-eyed and golden-haired, and a beauty. If we may credit
the thinly veiled hints of certain contemporaries, Grisi was
Gautier's mistress, but later abandoned him for several other
lovers, when the poet consoled himself with Mlle. Forster.
There exists a very charming poem by Gautier entitled *A la
Princesse Bathilde*, which begins by describing the advent of
dawn and the melting away of the pale Wilis, and the disappearance of Giselle into the flower-covered ground, then concludes
with an account of the arrival of Bathilde (Mlle. Forster), whose
praises are sung in the following lines :

" . . . Alors vous paraissez, chasseresse superbe,
 Trainant votre velours sur le velours de l'herbe,
 Un sourire à la bouche, un rayon dans les yeux,
 Plus fraîche que l'aurore éclose au bord des cieux ;

---

[1] *Op. cit.*, Vol. II, p. 139.
[2] Lifar (Serge), *op. cit.*, Appendix.

Belle au regard d'azur, à la tresse dorée,
Que sur ses blancs autels la Grèce eût adorée ;
Pur marbre de Paros, que les Grâces, en chœur,
Dans leur groupe admettraient pour quatrième sœur.
. . . De la forêt magique illuminant la voûte,
Une vive clarté se répand, . . . et l'on doute
Si le jour, qui renaît dans son éclat vermeil,
Vient de votre présence ou s'il vient du soleil !
Giselle meurt ; Albert éperdu se relève,
Et la réalité fait envoler le rêve ;
Mais en attraits divins, en chaste volupté,
Quel rêve peut valoir votre réalité ! "

* *
*

Joseph Lucien Petipa, known as Lucien Petipa, the creator of
Albrecht, was born at Marseille on December 22nd, 1815. His
father, Jean Petipa, who was both *premier danseur* and *maître de
ballet* to the Théâtre Royal de la Monnaie, Brussels, initiated him
in the art of dancing. Although Lucien made good progress,
his father delayed his *début*, while awaiting a favourable moment.

At this time a well-known Paris singer, Lafonte, who had
been enthusiastically received in Brussels, announced a benefit
performance at the Monnaie ; the house was soon sold out.
Jean Petipa seized the opportunity afforded and not only arranged
that his son should appear in the programme, but that he should
dance with Mlle. Ambrosini, a dancer well known to Brussels
theatre-goers. Lucien made a distinct success and the director
of the Theatre Royal, The Hague, who was among the audience,
immediately offered him a contract as *premier danseur* to that
theatre.

He danced at the Hague for three months and then obtained
a new engagement at the Grand Theatre, Bordeaux, at which
he charmed everyone with the lightness, gaiety, and precision
of his dancing. Now and again famous *danseuses* visited Bordeaux, including Fanny Elssler and the sisters Noblet, who,
delighted with Lucien's ability, urged him to go to Paris.

At first he hung back, fearing to risk his Bordeaux reputation
in the more critical and more difficult atmosphere of the French
capital. But at last he put his doubts aside and on arriving in
Paris was pleasantly surprised to find that his reputation had
preceded him. He soon obtained an engagement at the Opera

as *premier danseur de demi-caractere*, which would correspond nowadays to *premier danseur classique*, at which theatre he made his *début* on June 10th, 1840, appearing in *La Sylphide* with Fanny Elssler in the title-rôle. That was the beginning of a long sequence of successes in which he danced variously with Carlotta Grisi, Adelina Plunkett, Amalia Ferraris, and Carlotta Rosati.

He was Grisi's partner when she created the principal rôles in *Giselle*, *La Jolie Fille de Gand* (1842), *La Péri* (1843), *Le Diable à Quatre* (1845), *Paquita* (1846), *Griseldis* (1848), and *La Filleule des Fées* (1849). He also partnered Sofia Fuoco in *Betty* (1848), Carolina Rosati in *Jovita* (1853), and Amalia Ferraris in *Les Elfes* (1856) and *Marco Spada* (1857).

A lithograph of Lucien Petipa dated 1842 enables us to form an impression of his appearance a few months after his creation of the rôle of Albrecht. It shows a handsome young man in private dress. He is slender and well formed, and wears his well-fitting clothes with distinction. His head is well poised, the smooth, luxuriant hair dressed in the romantic coiffure typical of the period. His features are regular and pleasant, with large, intelligent eyes, aquiline nose, and small mouth with full lips, and a dimpled chin. His hands are small and delicate, almost feminine in their refinement.

Lucien made his first essay at choreography in 1853 when he produced the *divertissement* in Niedermeyer's opera, *La Fronde*. This was well received and in 1854 he was appointed a *maître de ballet*. In this capacity he began with a series of *divertissements* for various operas, for Gounod's *La Nonne Sanglante* (1854), for Verdi's *Les Vêpres Siciliennes* (1855), and for Auber's *Le Cheval de Bronze* (1857).

In 1858 he produced his first ballet, *Sacountala*, in two acts, with theme by Gautier and music by Ernest Reyer. The title-rôle was danced by Ferraris. This was followed by *Graziosa* (1861) and *Le Roi d'Yvetot* (1865). From then onwards, apart from a few *divertissements* for operas, he seems to have abandoned the composition of ballets and devoted himself to the fashioning of dancers. In 1860 he had been appointed " professor of the perfection class " and in 1865 he became principal *maître de ballet*. Several of his pupils attained distinction, among them being Louis Mérante. In 1868, Lucien injured his foot as the result of an accident, and, as his recovery was contingent on a long period of rest, he was obliged to resign his post.

Later he became professor of mime at the Conservatoire

National de Musique, and in 1880 was recalled to the Opera in the same capacity. In 1882, seventeen years after his last ballet, he produced *Namouna*, with book by Charles Nuitter—the author of *Coppélia*—and music by E. Lalo. The title-rôle was taken by Rita Sangalli. This ballet was the most successful of all his compositions, due, however, to certain of the dances rather than to the conception of the ballet as a whole.

Lucien Petipa died at Versailles on July 7th, 1898.

CHAPTER IX

THE CHARACTERS IN " GISELLE "

THERE are eight characters in Giselle, four male, and four female. These differ considerably in importance and may be divided into three groups : principal, secondary, and subsidiary.

There is only one principal rôle, that of Giselle, thus the ballet follows the prototype of *La Sylphide* by concentrating the supreme interest in the *ballerina*. But, in *Giselle*, Gautier, with his vivid memories of both Marie Taglioni and Fanny Elssler, the respective priestesses of the two rival domains of the Romantic Ballet, its ethereal and its earthly aspects, succeeded in combining these two opposed characteristics, previously always found separated, into one ballet. Thus the first act is a rôle for a dancer of the intelligence and mimetic power of Elssler, while the second is a part for a dancer like Taglioni, endowed with a phantom-like lightness and rare powers of elevation.

There are four secondary rôles, those of Albrecht, Hilarion, Myrtha, and Berthe, Giselle's mother, which order corresponds to their importance.

Finally, there are the three subsidiary rôles of Bathilde, the Prince of Courland, and Wilfrid.

In plays intended to be spoken and acted, it has been for many years the frequent and helpful practice for the playwright, when setting out his list of characters, to describe, with the intimate knowledge he alone can possess, the physical appearance, pyschological qualities, and other characteristics peculiar to each rôle, thus enabling the interpreter of the character and the producer of the piece to form some idea of the character of person the author had in mind.

The writers of stories for ballets, however, having set down the name of the character, content themselves with such curt observations as " a peasant," " a gamekeeper," and so forth. Hence, when taking a rôle in one of the classics of choreography, the dancer must either imitate to the best of her ability what is presumed to be the traditional rendering of the character, or apply herself to a study of the rôle in question with a view to presenting her own conception, within the confines of the traditional mime and choreographic script.

It is, perhaps, not unprofitable to speculate on the various characters in *Giselle*. Consider, first, the title-rôle. Of Giselle we know little more than that she is " a peasant," we must therefore try and visualise her from such clues as may be afforded by a study of the plot. Is Giselle a normal, well-set-up young village maiden, with more than her share of good looks? Pretty, no doubt, but hardly normal, her whole behaviour in various circumstances suggests quite the opposite. Even her own mother regards her daughter as something of an enigma. Is she not always scolding Giselle because of her mad craze for dancing, and warning her that if she does not take care she will kill herself, and, when she is dead, become a Wili ?

When Giselle makes light of her mother's fears, the latter explains to Loys, her daughter's sweetheart, that she is only warning Giselle for her own good, out of regard for her health, nay, her very life. " Giselle has always been delicate," her mother continues, " and the doctor told me that too much exercise or any over-excitement might be fatal to her."

Let us pass to the prelude to the Mad Scene. At this moment Giselle is rapturously happy in Loys's love. But when Loys is denounced by Hilarion and found to be already betrothed to the Princess Bathilde, Giselle becomes almost hysterical with rage and throws herself to the ground. A little later she staggers to her feet and is seen to be bereft of her reason. Quick temper and poor health might explain her frenzy and her tears, but for madness to result from what at worst is no more than a bitter disappointment, proves that Giselle must have been highly neurotic. What has Albrecht done ? Certainly he is guilty of having trifled with her affections, being already affianced to another, and of having pretended to be a peasant when he is in fact a nobleman, but that is all. There is no evidence to show that he was a potential or successful seducer, and while, in the game of love, a nobleman may find it helpful to masquerade as a peasant, it is not unknown for a villager to attempt to further his courting by boasting of riches which exist only in his imagination.

I have referred to Giselle's mother's being puzzled by her daughter, who resembles her in nothing. Instead of being robust and industrious, she is sickly and obsessed with a craze for dancing, a strange elfin creature whose shy, sensitive nature is so different from that of the light-hearted young girls of the district. This innate shyness and delicacy are revealed in all her love scenes with Loys.

Is Giselle step-child or foundling? If the former, Berthe would surely be described as her step-mother, or, in the latter case, as her foster-mother; but, as already stated, Berthe is definitely styled " Giselle's mother." Who was the father of Giselle? We do not know, for he never appears. Is Giselle's mother a widow, or has her husband deserted her? Is Giselle her natural rather than her lawful daughter? If the former, was the father commoner or nobleman? On all these matters the authors are silent and we can only rashly conjecture. But, were Giselle a natural daughter and her father of gentle birth, it would explain much.

Is Giselle dark or fair? Most Giselles have been dark and perhaps that colour is best suited to the rôle, for it affords greater mystery and wistfulness to the features. On the other hand, it may be recalled that Carlotta Grisi, the creator of the rôle, was, to quote Gautier, " fair, or at least light chestnut."

Some years ago I wrote a small monograph on Markova, and, in discussing her interpretation of the title-rôle of *Giselle*, I said that this ballet was to the dancer what *Hamlet* is to the actor. For, just as every actor aspires to play the name-part in *Hamlet*, so it is the ambition of every dancer to interpret the rich and varied rôle of Giselle. But, apart from the common importance of these two great rôles, is there not a parallel between the madness of Ophelia and that of Giselle? Both are the outcome of the bitter shock of thwarted love on a frail body inhabited by a hypersensitive nature.

To sum up, on the evidence available it is a reasonable deduction to assume that Giselle is young and pretty, but physically delicate, possibly large-eyed and pale-complexioned—a strange, complex being, paradoxically shy and simple, yet elusive and enigmatic, a restless, hypersensitive creature, introspective and essentially unworldly.

The chief of the secondary rôles and the principal male character is that of Albrecht. We know that he is a nobleman, the Duke of Silesia, and that, although betrothed to Bathilde, the Prince of Courland's daughter, he is in love with a peasant girl called Giselle. It is fair to conceive him as a handsome, well-proportioned young man, presumably in the twenties, whose gentle birth is reflected in his charming manners and graceful bearing. He is generally represented as clean-shaven, although some early interpreters of the rôle are portrayed wearing a moustache.

What is the character of Albrecht ? Is he, despite his pleasing exterior, merely an aristocratic libertine, who has assumed the humble name of Loys and appropriate peasant guise, in order to accomplish his evil design, or is he a man of honour who, having fallen in love with one of his tenants, and realising the immense distance which separates them on account of their difference in station, pretends to be one of her own class the better to gain her affection ? I incline to the latter view.

But, it may well be argued, if Albrecht is a man of honour, how does this accord with his making love to Giselle, when he is already betrothed to Bathilde ? It is possible that his engagement to Bathilde is not a true love match, but merely the prelude to a marriage of convenience, dictated by family or political considerations. It may be that, wearied of the artificialities of court life, he has sought true affection outside his own circle, and found it in the simple, shy love of Giselle.

The interpreter of Albrecht needs to be both graceful and manly, a rare combination ; a fine mime with a sensitive appreciation of style-atmosphere ; and an excellent *danseur classique*, for, although the major part of his rôle is concerned with miming and with partnering the *ballerina*, the one solo allotted to him, which occurs in the second act, includes several steps of exceptional difficulty. In brief, the appearance and bearing of Albrecht should be such that the eye always rests on him with delight. Finally, although he must support the *ballerina* to the utmost of his powers, he must never forget that there is only one principal rôle in this ballet, that of Giselle, and that any undue emphasis of his own importance would destroy the balance of the piece.

The rôle of Hilarion, which is all mime, is the one most frequently miscast, for, whether by accident or design, it is usually allotted to the most undersized male solo dancer in the company. Under these circumstances, Hilarion becomes an insignificant weakling, a nonentity. But surely the rivalry between Loys and Hilarion is the age-old contest between brain and brawn.

In the Middle Ages, when the forests were often infested with wolves and wild boars, the post of gamekeeper was hardly a sinecure. It would certainly not have been given to a weakling. On the contrary, I suggest that Hilarion is a sturdily built man of obvious peasant stock, in the late twenties or early thirties. His features would be weather-beaten from long hours in the open.

Since Albrecht is handsome, it is probable that the authors, in inventing Hilarion as a rejected lover who becomes a vindictive rival, would conceive him as being less favoured. Clearly he is a man of passionate nature and quick temper, as is proved by the development of the action. In this connection it is of interest to note that these qualities were once symbolised by his red beard, invariably worn in pre-1914 productions of *Giselle*, and which therefore may not unfairly be considered traditional.

One last point, a gamekeeper would enjoy a certain esteem in a hard-working peasant community. A man of this type would not fail to appeal strongly to the average village lass. That Giselle is made to reject his advances is, I submit, another indication of her variation from type.

Myrtha is the opponent of Giselle. Jilted by the man to whom she was betrothed, Myrtha died of grief in the flower of her youth. Presumably in her twenties, she would retain the age at which she became an immortal. But she is an unhappy phantom, a female vampire filled with an insatiable lust for revenge which causes her nightly to frequent the mystic glade, to lure any male wayfarer into the web of her fellow vampires, who force the unhappy man to dance until, reduced to exhaustion, he can be toppled to death in the marshy pool close by.

The rôle of Myrtha is practically all dancing and requires a soloist well equipped technically and possessed of an excellent *arabesque* and a good elevation. Myrtha is Queen of the Wilis. She must therefore radiate a certain authority and air of distinction which set her apart from her companions. Ideally considered, she should be beautiful in both face and form, yet with an icy coldness and air of melancholy about her which recall the tomb, for a vampire is a living corpse.

Berthe, Giselle's mother, is conceivably a woman in the forties. She would be of hard-working stock. It is not easy to divine her character with certainty. She is generally portrayed as slightly bent, surly, and perpetually scolding her daughter. But, setting aside her not unnatural dislike of Giselle's craze for dancing and aversion to work, there is no evidence that Berthe is a shrew. She might, with equal truth, be represented as a kindly, middle-aged woman[1], whose scolding arises simply from her maternal regard for her daughter's health. Hence the rôle of Berthe could be played in either way without affecting the development of the action.

Now we come to the subsidiary characters : Bathilde, the Prince of Courland, and Wilfrid. The first two are little more

---

[1] A good performance in this vein is that of Mme. Evina.

than conventional figures. Bathilde is a noble lady, a little older perhaps than Giselle. She is, I suggest, beautiful rather than pretty, and combines graciousness with dignity. The Prince of Courland is a middle-aged aristocrat of commanding presence. He is generally represented as wearing a well-trimmed moustache and beard.

Wilfrid, Albrecht's squire, although a minor rôle, is not without a certain importance. The style and dignity, or lack of them, with which the rôle is presented can easily make or mar the short but effective scenes between the squire and his master. With a few exceptions, the part of Wilfrid is badly played, the general conception corresponding to an obsequious servant, whose movements are frequently stiff and awkward. In these circumstances it may be helpful to discuss in detail the rank of squire.

The squire was the second stage in the mediæval school of chivalry which led to knighthood. But no youth became a squire before he had served some seven or eight years as page. He was almost invariably of gentle birth and entered on his duties at the age of eight or nine. During his apprenticeship as page, he was the constant personal attendant of both his noble master and mistress. He waited on them when they sat at meat, accompanied them when they went hunting, attended his mistress in her bower, and followed in his master's train when he went to war.

From his master and mistress and their retainers the page received instruction in the arts of polite behaviour, hunting, and hawking, and in the rudiments of military training. When promoted to squire, he continued the same duties, but now devoted more attention to the profession of arms, for, in time of war, the squire, unlike the page, was a combatant. When the squire was considered to have attained proficiency as a soldier, he became a squire of the body and in time of war fought by his master on the field of battle. Sometimes the squire left the service of his original master and attached himself to a young lord of his choice. After some years of faithful service the squire was promoted to knight.

But some squires, even when offered knighthood, declined the honour for lack of means to maintain the position. In this connection it is of interest to examine again the account of *Giselle* in *Les Beautés de l'Opéra*. The illustrations in the text suggest that the artist based his drawings on sketches made during an actual performance of the ballet at the Opera. In these

Wilfrid is represented as a man in the thirties with stern, bearded features. It is highly probable that originally Wilfrid was portrayed as an older man, for this would emphasise Albrecht's youth and confer additional dignity and dramatic effect in those scenes where the squire respectfully tenders his master advice which is curtly rejected—impetuous youth unheeding the voice of experience.

Present-day interpretations of the various characters discussed have, in more than one instance, strayed far from their original conception, so far as they can be built up from a study of the original synopsis and a consideration of the latent dramatic possibilities of a particular rôle. It is perhaps not too much to say that, were some of the lost details restored, the famous old ballet would further strengthen its hold on the affections of both public and artistes, an affection which it has maintained throughout a hundred years of performance.

CHAPTER X

THE ANATOMY OF " GISELLE "

SINCE the ardent concert-goer often finds that his appreciation of an orchestral work is increased by the study of a miniature score of the composition, it is reasonable to assume that the ballet-goer whose outlook is not confined to personalities may find it of equal benefit to study the anatomy or choreographic orchestration of *Giselle*. To this end I have placed after this chapter a choreographic script of both acts, based on the version given by the Markova-Dolin Ballet, as recorded by Molly Lake, a former member of that company[1] and now *maître de ballet* to the Ballet Guild. From this script I have prepared a simplified version which I must stress is not intended as a basis for performance[2] but solely for the use of the ballet-goer, who is expected to study it in conjunction with an actual performance or with his recollection of a performance. I have deliberately avoided a detailed explanation of all technical terms, some knowledge of which may be gained from a comparison of text with performance, or by consulting a work on ballet technique.

Viewed from a technical aspect, *Giselle* is composed of two elements—dancing and mime. In the first act, the mime consists of (*a*) short mimed scenes, and (*b*) episodes in which the mime is fused with the dancing. In the second act the mime is an integral part of the dancing.

An examination of the choreographic structure of *Giselle* reveals the interesting fact that the choreographers have been content to limit their palette to a comparatively small number of movements, steps, and poses familiar to students of classical ballet. These elements may roughly be classed[3] thus :

Movements : *développé, grand rond de jambe.*
Poses : *arabesque, attitude.*
Gliding steps : *chassé, glissade, pas de basque, pas de bourrée.*
Hopping steps : *ballonné, temps levé.*

---

[1] Miss Lake was the Myrtha in their production of *Giselle*.

[2] Among other things I have omitted some tiny links connecting the steps which, while vital to the dancer, would hardly be visible to the spectator, and I do not give the relation of the steps to the bars of the music.

[3] Some steps partake of more than one classification.

Leaping steps (vertical): *ballotté, entrechat, rond de jambe en l'air sauté, sissonne.*

Leaping steps (horizontal): *cabriole, jeté, grand jeté, soubresaut.*

Turning steps: *pirouette, petit tour, tour en l'air.*

These elements in various combinations and sequences are the basis of *Giselle*, and it must be admitted that they are used in masterly fashion, not only to provide an æsthetically pleasing composition, but also to express the development of the action and the varied situations that arise.

This calculated simplification of steps is doubtless intended to permit of the utmost expressiveness, at the same time this very simplicity concentrates critical attention on the dancers and demands from them the highest degree of technical execution and precision ; and yet the dancing must still appear spontaneous and not the fruits of a lesson well learned.

The tracks or linear ground patterns along which the dancers move are mainly straight lines, sometimes at right-angles to the audience, that is passing from 4—1, 3—2, or the reverse directions ; sometimes parallel to the audience, that is, passing from 2—1, 3—4, or 6—8, or the reverse directions ; or along the diagonals 3—1, 4—2, or the reverse directions.

Reference has been made to the expressiveness of the dancing ; two examples will serve to illustrate this fact. Note, for instance, in the first act, when Giselle and Loys express their mutual love in a *pas de deux*, that they waft silent kisses to each other during a *glissade à l'arabesque*. Similarly, in the second act, Giselle throws her lover a flower while bounding in a *grand jeté*. This soaring step is used to suggest Giselle's phantom-like swiftness and lightness, and when the throwing of the flower coincides with the highest point of the leap, an extraordinary effect of ecstasy is achieved.

Another unusual feature of *Giselle* is the use of what might be termed choreographic *Leitmotiv*. When Giselle dances for the entertainment of her friends, she expresses her delight in dancing by means of a series of *ballonnés piqués* followed by *pas de basque*. Later, when Bathilde asks Giselle what is her chief delight and receives the reply, " My heart's delight is to dance," Giselle gives choreographic expression to her joy by again dancing a series of *ballonnés piqués* followed by *pas de basque*. Again, in the Waltz, when Giselle and Albrecht dance together surrounded by their friends, at one time they do a series of *ballonné—chassé—coupé*, each making a beckoning movement with the raised arm on the *ballonné*. It conveys very successfully a suggestion of mutual happiness. Later, when Giselle has lost her reason, and believes herself still dancing with her beloved Loys, the choreographer makes Giselle repeat the same *enchaînement*, which is now danced slowly and jerkily to indicate the conflict between her mind and her limbs, and evokes a profound feeling of pity in the spectator. This affords a most interesting example of how the expressive potentialities of an *enchaînement* can be varied according to its manner of execution and timing.

The mimetic part of the first act consists in the main of short, crisp episodes, the meaning of which is probably sufficiently plain to the average ballet-goer. In ballet there are two kinds of mime, the Italian school, a vocabulary of stylised gestures of the hands and arms which probably goes back to the days of Bathyllus and Pylades, and the freer, natural style evolved by Michel Fokine, who required that the whole body should be expressive. In *Giselle* the miming is of course in the Italian tradition. Something of its principles may be gleaned from an examination of a few typical scenes.

1. *Hilarion goes to the door of Giselle's cottage and indicates it to be the abode of the person he loves.* To convey this, he mimes : There lives—the one—I—love. That is, he points to the cottage with his right hand, raises the index finger of the same hand vertically upwards, touches his chest with the finger-tips of both hands, then presses both hands to his heart.

2. (*a*) *Loys declares his love for Giselle and swears eternal fidelity*. To convey this, he mimes : I—you—love—I swear it. That is, he places both finger-tips to his breast, points to Giselle, presses both hands to his heart, then raises his right hand, index-finger extended vertically upwards, at the same time gazing upwards.

(*b*) *Giselle begs him not to swear fidelity*. To convey this, she lightly grasps Loys's upraised hand and quietly draws it downwards, at the same time shaking her head.

3. *Hilarion accuses Loys and Giselle of kissing and embracing.* To convey this, he mimes : You (Loys)—and you (Giselle)—have been kissing—and embracing. That is, he points with his right hand to Loys, then with his left hand to Giselle, kisses the back of his right hand, next, the back of his left hand, and then hugs himself.

4. *Giselle's mother warns her daughter that if she will persist in dancing she will die and become a Wili.* To convey this, she mimes : You will persist in dancing—you will die—you will become a Wili. That is, she arches her arms above her head and, wreathing

one hand about the other, gradually extends and raises them vertically upwards ; at the apex of the movement she clenches her fists and, crossing her wrists, lowers her arms straight in front of her, then, just as the arms fall vertically downwards, she unclenches her hands and sharply separates them ; she then turns sideways to the audience and, placing the backs of her wrists at the base of her spine, lightly flutters the hands.

5. *Bathilde, attracted by Giselle, praises the girl's beauty to her father.* The beauty of another person is always indicated by lightly passing one's hand in a circular clockwise movement about one's face.

6. *Loys signs to Bathilde to be silent.* To convey this, he mimes : You—be silent. That is, he extends his right hand towards her, then places the index finger of the same hand to his lips.

The second act, as we have seen, originally began with a series of apparitions, in which Wilis were seen flying over the misty pool, soaring from tree to tree, or suddenly appearing from, or vanishing into, a clump of wild flowers or a curtain of leaves. These effects were not danced, but the result of carefully planned stage effects—suggestions of flying by means of wires, optical illusions, and the simple but effective see-saw device illustrated in the plate facing page 63.

Having demonstrated the fertility of his mechanical invention, Perrot then proceeds to show that he can not only emulate such effects by persons dancing, but even surpass them, for, after this brief introduction, the whole of the act is danced from beginning to end, and balanced ideally between the poles of expressive dancing and danced mime. In no other ballet are the intermingled themes of the love of man for woman and the conflict between inexorable duty and the power of love treated with such refinement, lyricism, and delicate appreciation of the issues involved. This act, danced by artists, can be a genuine choreographic poem.

It is of interest to note how the familiar pose *arabesque* is inseparably associated with the Wilis, to become, as it were, their choreographic sign manual. Myrtha's opening solo sketches the use of the *arabesque*, and when her summoned band of Wilis perform their dance of incantation, the *arabesque* is used in a variety of ways, sometimes as the pose in which a step is danced, sometimes to conclude a phrase of steps. One very attractive combination is that produced by ranging the Wilis in two groups facing each other at right-angles to the audience on the lines 1—4 and 2—3, and then making them dance towards and through each other by a series of *temps levés en arabesque*. Again, when Giselle emerges from the tomb and becomes a Wili by Myrtha's touching her with her magic branch, she signifies her adherence by a rapturous series of *temps levés en arabesque en tournant*.

These *arabesques* are all *en l'air*, when the rear leg is raised to the fourth position *en l'air* ; but the *arabesque à terre*, in which the rear leg is not raised, but extended in the fourth position back, *pointe tendue*, is also frequently used. It is the pose almost invariably assumed by the Wilis when not actually dancing. When Hilarion finds himself hemmed in by the Wilis, each group stands in *arabesque à terre*, with the sole difference that the front arm, instead of being extended, is raised vertically upwards in a gesture of negation. The *arabesque à terre* is also the pose used by the Wilis when Hilarion goes to the Queen and entreats her mercy. And when the Wilis endeavour to force Albrecht from the shelter of the cross, only to recoil from its radiance, they again stand in *arabesque à terre*, but with one hand raised to shield their eyes.

There are several *adages* in this act, and among the most beautiful is that danced by Giselle when supported by Albrecht, a danced duet which expresses the strength of their love despite the efforts of the Wilis to part them. The dance consists mainly of full and expressive *développés*, in which the *ballerina* uses her body as a mute instrument of song. After the *développés* she passes *à l'arabesque*, and Albrecht, holding her by the waist, sways her gently to and fro in that position. Done with feeling, this sway can convey the languor of intense passion. This sway is succeeded by a leap upwards *en arabesque*, in which position she is held shoulder-high by Albrecht, as though restraining the flight of his beloved phantom, then he lowers her gently to the ground *en arabesque*, when she places her hand on his shoulder in a gesture of ineffable tenderness.

Another, later, solo by Giselle is notable for the brilliant *enchaînement* which brings it to an end, a series of sixteen *entrechats*[1] *quatre en diagonale*, which, when danced with ease and brilliance, suggest that the dancer is skimming, bird-like, just above the ground.

Apart from the meeting of the huntsmen at the beginning of the scene and the final " curtain," only three mortals appears in this act : Hilarion, Wilfrid, and Albrecht. Of these, Albrecht

---

[1] Some dancers substitute the easier *changement* for the *entrechat*.

alone dances. The principal steps allotted to him are the *ballotté, cabriole,* and *tour en l'air,* all steps of elevation, and the *pirouette* ; all these are used to suggest Albrecht's enforced dancing at Myrtha's command and his initial exhilaration and subsequent exhaustion. These effects are suggested by increasing or decreasing the height of the leaps, and by increasing or decreasing the velocity of the turning movements.

But there are so many lovely things in this act, which is virtually a long *pas de deux* between Giselle and Albrecht, that, in the short space of a chapter, one can do no more than select a few examples and offer them for consideration. A whole volume could be devoted to an examination of the second act alone.

One word more. An unusual feature of this second act, probably unique at this period, is the manner in which the dancing of the *corps de ballet* and soloists is combined to form one whole. The *corps de ballet* is never employed as a mere decorative background, but as an integral part of the ballet, sometimes dancing apart, sometimes dancing with the principals, but always making an essential and vital contribution both to the choreographic design and to the development of the action.

CHAPTER XI

THE curtain rises on an empty stage. A number of peasant
girls enter at 3. They arrive in twos and threes, talking
and beckoning to one another, then exit slowly at 4, behind
Giselle's cottage, at left.

As girls exit, Hilarion enters at 3. He goes to door of Giselle's
cottage and indicates it to be the abode of the person he loves.
He is about to knock when, hearing approaching footsteps, he
conceals himself behind the cottage.

Enter Albrecht at 3, attended by his squire, Wilfrid. That
the former is a person of rank is denoted by his rich cloak and
plumed barret, and the sword at his belt. Albrecht goes towards
the other cottage at right. As he nears the door he takes off
his barret and cloak and gives them to his squire, who follows
him in as he enters the cottage, unbuckling his sword-belt.
Presently Albrecht emerges, dressed in peasant clothes. He
goes towards Giselle's cottage, followed by his squire, who
seems to be dissuading him from some project, but Albrecht
abruptly dismisses Wilfrid, who, bowing low, takes his departure.
Albrecht again goes towards the door of Giselle's cottage, knocks,
listens, then mimes " here she comes " and hides behind bush
at 4.

Giselle opens the door and steps out, then, dancing lightly,
circles about the stage to R. with a series of *glissade—chassé—
ballonné devant*. Returning to centre, she expresses surprise that,
although someone knocked, the glade is empty. Dismissing
the matter with a shrug of her shoulders, she resumes her dance
until, hearing the sound of kisses blown to her by Albrecht[1],
she stops in a listening attitude. Conscious of Albrecht's presence, she tries to find him, but failing to do so, gives a petulant
stamp of her foot and backs to centre to collide with Albrecht,
who, tired of teasing, has come to greet her.

Now follows a little amorous by-play in which Albrecht

---

[1] Although, as the reader is aware, Albrecht is known to Giselle by his
assumed name of Loys, I have here referred to him throughout as Albrecht,
for the sake of clarity.

nudges Giselle's shoulder, to which she replies with a modest curtsey. Then, overcome with shyness, she flees to her cottage, hotly pursued by Albrecht, who gently draws her back. She makes a little *balancé* movement while he does so. This incident is repeated several times with variations in detail, when Albrecht slips her arm through his and leads her into a series of gliding steps (*glissades changés*). Then Giselle passes in front of Albrecht and, spreading her skirts, sits on the rustic bench. Albrecht asks her to make room for him, which she does. But whenever he adroitly moves a little closer to her, she correspondingly edges away, then suddenly rises and runs to her cottage. But Albrecht bounds forward in pursuit and draws her back.

He declares his love for her and swears eternal fidelity. Giselle begs him not to swear affection and, running to the window-box of her cottage, followed by her lover, she plucks a marguerite. Then, beckoning to Albrecht, she glides to centre of stage and again sits on the bench. While Albrecht, resting one foot on the bench, watches her, she picks the flower petal by petal, saying, " he loves me," " he loves me not," nodding and shaking her head in turn. When the test appears to end in a negative she flings down the flower, runs near 8, and, falling on her knees, gives way to tears. Albrecht picks up the discarded flower and, continuing to pluck the petals, ends with " he loves me." Giselle, soothed and enraptured, takes Albrecht's arm and dances a few steps (series of *ballotté— coupé—ballonné—posé—jeté croisé*) with him. During this scene, Hilarion crosses back stage from 3, and, seeing Giselle dancing with Albrecht, shakes his fist in anger at him and runs off at 4.

The lovers end the *ballotté* step in the centre, when Albrecht begs Giselle to give him a kiss ; she laughingly refuses and evades his pursuit of her.

Giselle and Albrecht now dance in a circle to R., repeating this *enchaînement* 4 times : *glissade—jeté élancé en avant à l'arabesque,* then, kissing her R. finger, she lightly presses it on his brow, and, with a *dégagé* and *renversé* movement, runs to 4, where she is halted by the sudden entrance of Hilarion.

Confronting her with folded arms, he forces her back to centre with two heavy stamps of his foot. Albrecht walks to 1. Hilarion accuses the lovers of kissing and embracing, and reproves them for their behaviour. Giselle, furious, drives Hilarion back with two stamping steps. Hilarion, overcome by this rejection, falls on his knees and declares his love for her. Giselle mocks his overtures, laughs derisively, and turns her back on him.

Hilarion raises his fist as if to strike her, but Albrecht hurls him aside and bids him begone. He exits slowly at 3, shaking his fist at Albrecht and vowing vengeance. Albrecht runs to Giselle and clasps her in his arms, after which they walk to 2, as village girls, carrying baskets of grapes, enter at 4. They gather about Giselle, who asks them what they have been doing. When they reply that they have been gathering grapes, she bids them come and dance, an invitation they accept with alacrity. Setting down their baskets at back, they group themselves in a large semi-circle.

Waltz. Giselle and Corps de Ballet.

1. C. de B.   Six *balancés—soutenu* on points.   Repeat twice in all.

     Gis.   Travelling down centre, does 3 *ballonnés piqués devant* L—*pas de basque en l'air* to L., repeats to R., then 4 *balancés*. Repeats whole step.

2. C. de B.   *Temps levé en arabesque* to centre, *balancé en arrière*—repeat—3 *coupés ballonnés—pas de bourrée—relevé* on points. Repeats whole step, omitting *relevé*.

     Gis.   Steps on R. F., does *posé* L. point, *grand rond de jambe, tombé*. Repeats to opposite side, then, turning in small circle to her R., steps on R. point and does *double rond de jambe, plié*; this last is repeated 3 times in all. Now she repeats first half of step, replacing the *rond de jambe* with a *posé en arabesque*, after which she runs to Albrecht at 2 and invites him to dance.

3. C. de B.   Half girls of L. half of semi-circle join hands, half girls of R. half do the same. All do continuous waltz forward.

   G. & A.   Facing each other at 2, Albrecht holding Giselle's R. hand with his L., Albrecht facing 1, travels forward with 3 *ballonnés piqués—pas de basque*, while Giselle, her back to 1, moves backwards to 1, using same step. They circle to 4, changing hands as they do step to alternate sides, finally travelling forward arm-in-arm with series of *ballonnés devant*.

4. C. de B.   Two couples on L., one behind the other, and 2 couples on R., similarly arranged, cross each other, each couple faces centre. They do

	relevé in 1st pos. on points and drop in *demi-plié*, then repeat *relevé* dropping in *arabesque à terre*, and do 2 *ballonnés*. They repeat whole step travelling in opposite direction.
G. & A.	Albrecht in centre lifts Giselle vertically upwards, her feet being in 5th pos., her arms 5th *en haut*, then he lowers her to ground on points, when she leans to R., R. arm in half 5th *en haut*. Albrecht then travels to R., Giselle opposite him, doing *ballonné—chassé—coupé*, this step is repeated, after which they run to centre and repeat step from lift, but to opposite side.
5. C. de B.	Two girls at each corner, facing each other and holding R. hands, waltz forward turning, waving L. arms in and out over head. After 3 steps and a stamp of the feet, they change hands and reverse. They repeat the whole 3 times, then two smallest girls lead others— with a waltz step—into double diagonal on the line 1—3.
G. & A.	Giselle joins couple at 2 and does the same as they do. Albrecht joins couple at 4, and also does the same. Giselle goes to 1 and intimates that she will dance again. Albrecht goes to 3 and waits.
6. C. de B.	Girls remain in diagonal lines, R. F. 4th pos. back, *pointe tendue*.
Gis.	Travels towards 3 with 7 *posé* turns and *assemblé* to face 1, then, taking Albrecht's arms in hers, they do 3 *ballonnés piqués—pas de basque*, repeating this *enchaînement* 4 times to 1.
7. C. de B.	Still in double diagonal line, all step forward and do *relevé développé effacé*, then *plié* and *pas de bourrée en arrière* and *assemblé en tournant* to L. to face 2. The whole is repeated 3 times in all. They now face each other in 2 lines, joining R. hands in couples. They do 3 waltz steps forward, making half-turn, then *assemblé relevé* in 5th. They repeat from waltz step, turning back to original places, then 2 girls lead to big wheel, one going to 6, the other to 8. Half girls face 7, half face 5, standing in one straight line, arms about each other's waists.

8. G. & A.   Giselle goes to one end of the line, Albrecht to
             the other. All move together with 3 waltz
             steps, making ¼ turn to L., so that the line
             now runs from 6—8. This is repeated 4 times
             in all, so that the line, turning on an imaginary
             pivot, makes a complete revolution.

9. C. de B. Two girls in centre lead outwards so that one
             half of line goes to 2, the other half to 1. They
             then pass up stage, down stage, and up stage
             again to form a semi-circle with original centre
             couple back in their places.

   G. & A.   They wait at 3.

10. C. de B. They rest, feet in 4th pos., *pointe tendue*, arms
             demi-seconde pos. (Girls on spectator's L. half,
             point R.F.; those on spectator's R. half,
             point L.F.)

   G. & A.   Giselle does 2 *petits tours* on point from 3.
             Albrecht, walking behind her, lifts her vertically
             upwards. They repeat the whole, finishing
             centre, with Giselle sitting on Albrecht's knee,
             her R.F. forward and *pointe tendue*, her L.F.
             bent under her on point, her L. arm round
             his shoulders.

11. C. de B. Rest.

   G. & A.   They walk to 1, Giselle waits while Albrecht
             dances.

12. C. de B. Rest.

   A.   He, travelling back to centre, does *entrechat cinq*—
             *posé — dégagé — assemblé — sissonne ouverte — as-
             semblé* back. This is repeated 4 times in all,
             but, during the last repeat, *assemblé* is replaced
             by a *pas de bourrée* under.

13. C. de B. Rest.

   G. & A.   Albrecht finishes his *pas de bourrée* behind and to L.
             of Giselle, then takes her R.H. in his R.H.
             They do *ballonné—chassé—coupé*, making a
             beckoning movement with L. arm over head
             on *ballonné*. This step is repeated 3 times in
             all, travelling back to 3, then each does a *pas
             de bourrée*, Giselle's being on place so that
             Albrecht passes behind her. The whole is
             then repeated to opposite side 4 times in all
             and omitting the *pas de bourrée*.

14. C. de B.   Rest.
    G. & A.   Arm-in-arm and facing 5, do *coupé ballonné*—step
               forward—*jeté élancé à l'arabesque croisée*, the step
               being repeated 4 times in all to alternate sides.
15. C. de B.   Rest.
    G. & A.   Giselle circles up stage to R., Albrecht to L.
               Giselle does *glissade posé* on point in small
               arabesque. Albrecht does the same to the other
               side. They face each other across stage in
               these *arabesques*, blowing each other a kiss.
               This is repeated 8 times in all to alternate sides
               and meeting at 3. They now do same step
               to 1, Giselle facing front, Albrecht facing
               Giselle.
16. C. de B.   Rest.
    Gis.   She does 8 *posé* turns to 3 on L. point. Albrecht
               waits at 1, Giselle then does 4 *petits tours* to L.
               to centre, where she is met by Albrecht.
17. C. de B.   Keeping semi-circular formation, they do *temps
               levé*, then *chassé* to wings, slightly swinging
               arms and head. The whole is then repeated,
               then follows *temps levé en arabesque* to centre,
               coupé, and *assemblé*. The whole is again re-
               peated, then follow 2 turns and *pas de bourrée*
               on point on place, arms 5th *en haut*. Facing 5,
               they lower inside foot to 4th pos. back, *pointe
               tendue*, arms *demi-seconde* pos.
    G. & A.   In centre and facing 5, they do *entrechat trois*—
               glissade—*posé* on points in *attitude croisé*,
               Giselle facing 2 and Albrecht opposite. This
               is repeated 4 times travelling inwards, then,
               placing an arm about each other's waist, they
               turn to L. twice and end with Giselle sitting
               on Albrecht's knee, her L. arm round his
               shoulders, while he clasps her waist with both
               arms.

The door of Giselle's cottage opens and her mother, half
angry and half worried, comes bustling out. The girls, smiling,
crowd round her, so that Giselle can hide behind their skirts.
But her mother soon disperses them and drags Giselle from
their midst, exclaiming in horror at her daughter's flushed features.
She takes out her handkerchief, mops her daughter's brow,
smoothes her dress, and then inquires what she has been doing.

Giselle laughingly replies that she has been dancing, and, by way of demonstration, proceeds to do 3 *ballonnés—pas de basque*, travelling round stage.

Her mother stops her and warns Giselle that if she will persist in dancing, she will die and become a Wili. Her girl friends look on, half amused, half afraid.

The mother drives her daughter into the cottage. Unwilling, Giselle tries to return to her friends and Albrecht, but her mother pushes the girls aside and forces her daughter inside the cottage. Just as her mother is about to shut the door, she opens it slightly and shakes her fist at Albrecht.

The girls take up their baskets and exit at 4. Albrecht goes off at 2.

As the last girl exits, Hilarion enters at 3. He goes to Giselle's cottage and listens, but, disturbed by the sound of a distant hunting-horn, goes to 4. Seeing the approach of a hunting-party, he runs to Albrecht's cottage, where he hides.

Wilfrid enters at 4 and summons a number of huntsmen, who form a line from 4—3. Now come two ladies-in-waiting, followed by Bathilde and her father, the Prince of Courland. This last group stands at 2, facing 1. The Prince glances round while Wilfrid, at his command, knocks at Giselle's cottage.

The door is opened by the mother, who asks Wilfrid the reason for his visit. He indicates the Prince and Bathilde and explains that they desire rest and refreshment. The mother curtsies and, calling two girls from inside the cottage, bids them bring out a table and two stools, which they set before the cottage. Then they place a pitcher and goblets on the table.

Giselle emerges from the cottage and, noticing the unwonted activities, goes inquiringly to her mother, then, catching sight of Wilfrid, now standing centre, she curtsies to him. But the squire shakes his head and, indicating the Prince and Bathilde, explains that it is to them that homage should be paid. Bathilde, remarking Giselle, praises the girl's beauty to her father. Giselle goes to them, curtsies, and begs them to be seated at table. The Prince assents, and, taking Bathilde by the hand, leads her to the table at which they take their places, both facing the audience.

Wilfrid waits on the Prince and his daughter. Bathilde puts the goblet to her lips, and, in answer to her father's look of inquiry, expresses her satisfaction with the contents. Meanwhile Giselle steals timidly near Bathilde and, attracted by the silken sheen of her dress, kneels beside her and furtively fingers the material. Bathilde, touched by Giselle's artless pleasure in her dress, places a finger under her chin and bids her rise. Then she walks with her to centre and asks her the nature of her work. She replies that she spins and weaves. To this Bathilde replies, " and is that your heart's delight ? " " No," replies Giselle, " my heart's delight is to dance."

Then, as if to give visual expression to her words, Giselle begins to dance to her R. in a circle, using the step—3 *ballonnés piqués—grand pas de basque*, repeated 3 times in all and ending with a curtsey to Bathilde, who watches her with evident admiration. The Prince rises from table soon after Bathilde and strolls to 2. Giselle's mother stands near her cottage and, seeing her daughter dancing, expresses her disapproval, warning her that she will become a Wili, but Giselle pays no heed.

Bathilde goes to her father and, pointing to her necklace, earrings, and bracelet, asks his permission to present one of them to Giselle. On his assent, Bathilde takes off her necklace and beckons to Giselle. When she approaches, Bathilde places the necklace about Giselle's neck, whereupon the latter seizes her benefactor's hand and kisses it with fervent gratitude. Then Giselle runs to her mother and proudly displays Bathilde's gift, which her mother admires profusely.

Giselle then goes to the Prince and invites him to rest awhile in her cottage, which invitation he graciously accepts. Wilfrid opens the cottage door, bowing, as the Prince and Bathilde enter, followed by the two ladies-in-waiting, then by Giselle and her mother. The Prince then retraces his steps and returns to 2, where, summoning Wilfrid, he gives him his hunting-horn, instructing him to sound a call on it should his presence be required. Wilfrid, bowing low, takes the hunting-horn. The Prince crosses the stage and goes once more into Giselle's cottage. Wilfrid dismisses the huntsmen, who exit at 4, after which he hangs up the hunting-horn by the cottage door and departs in the same direction.

Hilarion emerges from Albrecht's cottage carrying a knightly sword. Pointing to the weapon, he indicates that he discovered it in the cottage, and that the sword shall be the instrument of his vengeance. He goes towards Giselle's door and is about to knock when he hears the voices of some approaching girls. He quickly runs to 4 and, seeing the girls, exits at 3.

The girls enter dancing, the principal steps used being *pas de basque*, *glissade*, *chassé*, and *temps levé en arabesque*. The dance ends with the girls running to Giselle's cottage and knocking at the door. When her mother appears, they beg her to allow Giselle to dance with them. At first she refuses, then finally consents. Giselle is lifted on to the table outside the cottage door and crowned with vine leaves as Queen of the Vintage. Then she springs to the ground and prepares to dance, while her friends group themselves in a semi-circle about her.

Solo : Giselle.

Giselle stands centre with L.F. in 4th pos. back, *pointe tendue*, arms *demi-seconde*, then she changes weight to L.F. so that R.F. is *pointe tendue*, at same time slightly extending her arms. Then she dances the following 4 steps :

1. *Glissade—posé* into *arabesque—demi-plié—posé* on point to 2 with *petit battement sur le cou-de-pied—posé* on point with *p.b.* on opposite foot—*posé* on point with *p.b.* as at first—*demi-plié* bringing the R.F. to *croisé devant—relevé* executing *grand rond de jambe en l'air en dehors—renversé—pas de bourrée en dehors*. Repeats whole step to opposite side replacing *grand rond de jambe renversé* with *posé* into *arabesque*, then runs to 2.

2. *Glissade* to 4—*posé en attitude* on point, passing R.F. to *pointe tendue* facing 2—*demi-plié—relevé*—passing working foot on slow *développé* to *arabesque*. Repeats whole step which brings Giselle to centre. *Glissade piqué—posé* on point—2 *tours en dedans*, arms 5th *en haut*—drops in 5th with arms extended towards her friends as though inviting their approval. Repeats from *glissade* to opposite side, she then does *temps levé en arabesque* and runs to 3 to stand on points in 5th pos., facing 2, with arms 4th *en avant*, R. arm across.

3. Series of hops on point—3 *ronds de jambe en l'air en dehors*— 3 hops bringing R.F. to *retiré*, L. arm across. Repeats these 2 movements 6 times in all, travelling diagonally to 1, then runs to 3 and stands with R.F. in 4th pos. front, *pointe tendue*, arms 4th *en avant*, L. arm across.

4. *Chassé—relevé—*1½ *tours en dedans* on point—*demi-tour en dehors* on point—*tombé—posé—tour en dehors* on point—*posé—* 1 *tour en dehors* on point. Repeats whole 3 times in all, with 4 *petits tours* at end at 1 and small *pas de chat* to 4, arms in 3rd *arabesque*.

Giselle's friends applaud her solo, then, forming a straight line in the centre, they dance an *ensemble*, towards the close of which they are joined by Giselle and Albrecht. The dance ends near the footlights with the happy laughing lovers clasped in each other's arms.

Suddenly, Hilarion enters at 3. Rushing down centre, he pushes the lovers apart. Then, turning to Giselle, he declares, " You may be engaged, but let me tell you that that man (pointing to Albrecht) is an impostor ! " Signing to Giselle to wait, he offers to bring proof. He runs off at 3 and returns bearing Albrecht's sword. Halting centre, he proffers it—hilt first— to Giselle for her inspection.

Wilfrid enters at 4 and asks Hilarion what he is doing, while Giselle regards the sword with the most casual interest. Hilarion, enraged, crosses to Giselle and, stressing the sword's costly hilt, points to Albrecht as the owner. Giselle pushes Hilarion aside and, going to Albrecht and putting her arm on his shoulder, asks him if the sword is his. He is silent and hangs his head, then, furious in his turn, Albrecht dashes at Hilarion and, dragging the sword from the scabbard grasped by the gamekeeper, is about to run him through when Wilfrid stays his arm. In the ensuing struggle the sword falls to the ground.

Giselle goes to her mother at 1, while Hilarion runs to the cottage door, seizes the hunting-horn and, despite Wilfrid's attempt to stop him, succeeds in blowing it.

The Prince emerges from the cottage, followed by Bathilde and her ladies. The Prince, recognising Albrecht, draws his daughter's attention to his presence and to his strange manner of dress. She goes to Albrecht and inquires what is the matter. He replies, " Nothing," and, dropping on one knee, kisses her hand. Giselle, who has watched this episode with growing uneasiness, forces herself between them and asks Albrecht what he is about. Albrecht is silent. Then Giselle turns to Bathilde and asks : " Are you his betrothed ? " Albrecht signs to Bathilde to be silent, but, too late, she inclines her head in assent.

Giselle, in a frenzy, tears off the necklace presented to her by Bathilde and flings it to the ground, then she runs to her mother and throws herself, face downwards, at her feet, sobbing with anguish. Albrecht runs to her side and, kneeling, tries to calm her, while her friends gather about her in mingled amazement and pity. Her mother, kneeling beside Giselle, loosens her hair. But, in a new fit of despair, she flings up her head and arms, only to collapse afresh. After a short pause, she again raises her head and arms, only to collapse again. The company start back in horror on each of these movements, on the last of which Albrecht crosses to 2.

Giselle, rising with difficulty to her feet, her reason gone, wanders slowly in a circle to her L., then, coming down centre, she pauses, placing first one hand then the other over her eyes in a gesture of bewilderment. She then makes a vague, appealing gesture first with one hand, then with the other, and goes to 2, where it is evident from her actions that uppermost in her confused thoughts is the memory of the dawn of her love for Albrecht. Kneeling, she picks an imaginary marguerite, and begins to detach the petals, whispering, " he loves me," " he loves me not.". . .

Staggering to her feet, she walks slowly in a circle, her arms hanging listlessly at her side. As she arrives at centre her foot comes into contact with Albrecht's sword, which still lies where it had fallen. With an unexpected exultant gleam in her eyes, she seizes the sword near its point and backs slowly to 3, trailing the hilt over the ground ; the onlookers recoil in horror. Then she goes to 1, lifting the sword from the ground, and, as she crosses, with a sudden movement she forces the sword-point into her breast. Albrecht, who till then has remained motionless with apprehension, hurries forward to take the sword from her, but too late. He runs to 1, followed by Giselle, who falls into her mother's arms. Albrecht, passing behind them, gives the sword to a huntsman standing near by.

Giselle struggles from her mother's arms and runs to attack Bathilde at 3. Her father raises his arm to protect her, but Giselle never reaches her objective. Half-way across, she turns back to her mother, while the Prince with Bathilde and her ladies exit slowly at 4.

Giselle turns to Albrecht and invites him to dance. He hastens to her side, only to realise from her dazed expression that he has become a complete stranger to her. But Giselle, fondly imagining that she is dancing with her lover as of old, falters through that familiar step—*ballonné en arrière—glissade* with a beckoning movement of her trembling hand. This step is done 4 times, then repeated similarly to the opposite side.

Now the familiar melody of the step she danced with her lover echoes in her bemused brain. Twice she listens intently to this phrase, then pitifully tries to dance the accompanying step : *coupé* L.—*ballonné* R.—step on R.F.—*jeté croisé* with L.F.

Her movements become weaker and weaker as her strength gradually ebbs away. She places her hands to her breast, then clasps her cheeks and strokes her hands. Alarmed by the icy coldness that is stealing over her, she stumbles along the fringe of frightened onlookers, looking for someone to help her. She staggers towards her mother and falls at her feet. Her mother, overcome with grief, kneels beside her daughter and tries to soothe her. Giselle half raises herself, then beckons to Albrecht at 2. He comes and kneels close to her, when she gently touches his cheeks in token of loving forgiveness and falls back—dead. During this scene the bystanders, deeply stirred, draw near to the tragic figure of their dying friend.

Albrecht raises Giselle's arm, but realising that she is dead, allows it to fall back. Hilarion, who is in the centre of the crowd, runs to 2, where he kneels and offers up a fervent prayer. Albrecht, catching sight of the gamekeeper, drags him to face Giselle's lifeless body, bidding him gaze on his handiwork, then hurls him aside. Hilarion staggers to 2 and falls to the ground. Albrecht snatches his sword from the huntsman to whom he had confided it, and lifts it in the air to cut down Hilarion, but again Wilfrid springs forward and stays his arm. Albrecht drops the sword and, pushing his squire aside, kneels once more beside his dead sweetheart. The onlookers draw closer in varied attitudes of sorrow, some standing, some kneeling. The men doff their caps.

The curtain falls in complete silence.

CHAPTER XII

THE two acts into which *Giselle* is divided might well be entitled : I. The Sword; II. The Cross; so great is the influence of these two objects upon the development of the plot. In fact, the whole meaning of the ballet depends upon the proper appreciation of their significance. There is, too, a fortuitous, even if unintentional, association in these two objects, for an inverted sword, that is, one held upright, with the hilt uppermost, becomes a cross.

Before discussing the action of Act I, let us consider the setting. The main features of the scene are two cottages, that of Giselle to the spectator's left, that of Loys to the right, with a vineyard in the middle distance, and, dominating the horizon, a rocky height crowned with a feudal castle. This turretted keep provides another touch of symbolism, for Loys, or to give him his true name, Albrecht, resides there, and so throughout the scene the castle is at once a reminder of Loys's noble birth and of the difficulty of bridging the gap between castle and cottage, for at this period the feudal lord was king over all who dwelt within his domain.

It is not easy to arrange these two cottages so that the game-keeper, Hilarion, can spy upon Albrecht and his squire going to the former's cottage, while remaining in concealment unseen either by them or by Giselle, should she chance to look out of the window of her abode. Quite often, when the stage is small, Loys's cottage is omitted altogether, which must make the subsequent proceedings quite incomprehensible to anyone seeing the ballet for the first time.

It cannot be over-emphasised that the entire understanding of Act I depends upon the manner in which the episode of Hilarion's spying upon Loys is presented. When the peasant girls have crossed in little groups from one side of the stage to the other, the scene is momentarily empty. Then Hilarion enters and peers about him as if in search of someone. He gazes at Giselle's cottage with tenderness and at its neighbour with anger. Albrecht approaches, richly dressed, accompanied by his squire, Wilfrid. They enter the hut to the right. Hilarion, his suspicions aroused, hides and watches. Presently, Wilfrid emerges and is seen conversing with Albrecht, now dressed as the peasant, Loys. The former seems to be urging the latter to abandon some project. He is dismissed, but bows low before taking his departure. Hilarion, not unnaturally, is puzzled that so well-dressed a youth should pay homage to a peasant. Few producers realise how vital is this incident to the under-standing of the subsequent action, yet it is frequently regarded as a mere preamble to the ballet and presented so carelessly, that it either passes unnoticed or produces but the most fleeting impression.

The whole purpose of this short scene is to inform the audience that Loys, although dressed as a peasant, is really a nobleman in disguise. The best setting for Act I in relation to this particular episode was that designed by Léon Zack for the production made by Boris Romanov for the National Ballet of Lithuania, which was seen in London during February, 1935, when that company gave a short season at the Alhambra Theatre.

In this setting the impression of a mountainous locality was conveyed by placing Giselle's cottage and Loys's abode at the base of a steep incline ; on the farther side of each cottage ran a flight of crude steps, cut in the bank, which led to an overhead horizontal path running at the base of a still taller hill. This arrangement afforded opportunity for the action to take place on several planes.

The next episode, in which Loys woos Giselle, is sometimes misplayed. Loys, despite his peasant dress, must certainly betray his noble birth in his every gesture, his graceful bear-ing, and charming manners. Obviously, there can be no suggestion of a son of the soil making love to a village lass. Yet what could be more banal that those noisy kisses with which Loys informs Giselle of his presence, or their accidental meeting, effected by making them collide back to back.

And what of Giselle herself ? Surely her whole attitude towards her sweetheart Loys is that of a shy, innocent young girl's first awakening to love. The moments when she evades Loys's attempt to hold her hand by running towards the safety of her cottage, are merely the instinctive reactions of a shy nature seeking escape in flight. But so often this scene is mimed with more than a hint of sophisticated coquetry. The manner in which this incident is played will do much to establish the quality of the performance to be expected from the respective interpreters of Giselle and Loys.

Then comes the charming scene in which Giselle makes her artless trial of Loys's love by the plucking of flower petals. This episode is doubtless borrowed from Goethe's *Faust*, in which Marguerite makes the same trial of Faust's love. In some productions of *Giselle* one flower only is used ; Giselle plucks the flower petal by petal, miming the time-honoured words, " he loves me," " he loves me not." But, before the petals are exhausted, she flings the flower to the ground in despair, whence it is retrieved by Loys, who continues the test with complete success. This method is open to criticism, for, if Giselle discards the flower before the test has been carried to its logical conclusion, that is, before all the petals have been plucked, it is inconclusive and unsatisfactory. This scene is best played with two flowers. Giselle plucks the petals from one blossom and lets fall the second with the cry, " he loves me not." Then Loys picks up the second flower and, plucking the petals himself, contrives to pass the test with success. One last point, it is essential that the petals be made of paper and easily detachable, for nothing so quickly destroys the romantic mood of this episode than to witness Giselle tugging and wrenching at each petal in order to remove it.

When Loys has convinced Giselle of his fidelity, they express their joy in a dance. In the Romanov production to which I have referred, the choreographer, in an endeavour to stress the rustic nature of the dance, struck an original note by making both dancers wear heeled shoes, thus the *pas de deux* became a character number, based, moreover, on country dance steps. As if to still further emphasise its rustic character, the dance ended with both dancers simultaneously dropping to the ground in a sitting position. It was an interesting experiment, but it made the dance seem crude and coarse, completely destroying the romantic mood which is the very essence of the ballet.

A little later, when Giselle's friends arrive with baskets to gather the grapes, the distant tra-la-la of hunting-horns announces the imminent arrival of a hunting-party. Loys, a little alarmed at the prospect of visitors, seeks escape by leading the girls to their work in the vineyards, while Giselle and her mother go into the cottage.

It is at this point that Hilarion returns and, seeing the coast clear, takes the opportunity to enter Loys's hut. Quite often he enters the hut as casually as though he were entering his own home. But if this situation is to have any dramatic value, surely there should be at least a hint of forcible entry. Could he not climb through the window, or force the door with the blade of his hunting-knife ? And when he does emerge with Albrecht's knightly sword and mantle, it is essential that these articles should be clearly visible to the audience. A stage direction in the musical score says, " Hilarion hides the sword and mantle in a bush." Thus he has the incriminating evidence ready at hand to produce at the psychological moment. In early productions, Hilarion carried a third symbol, the golden spurs of knighthood, a contemporary omission which might well be restored. In the 1863 revival at the Paris Opera, the incriminating evidence consisted of a richly-plumed cap, a gold-hilted sword, and a heavy gold chain.

I have already mentioned the importance of representing Loys's cottage, because, without it, this important stage in the action cannot be presented. When Loys's cottage is omitted, Hilarion goes into the fields—represented by the wings—to return bearing a sword and mantle which he intimates are the property of Loys. What evidence is there to connect with Loys a sword and mantle presumably found by chance in the fields ? Indeed, it is not impossible that Hilarion might have placed such articles there himself.

While Hilarion is engaged in trespass, the hunting-party, led by the Prince of Courland and his daughter, Bathilde, enter. Then follows the charming scene of the Prince and his daughter taking refreshments served by Giselle and her mother. Giselle, while standing behind Bathilde, is attracted by the latter's dress, which, to her simple eyes, seems to be made of fairy-like material. Cat-like, she bends down to examine the dress more closely and, unable to withold her curiosity and admiration, fearfully touches the material with the tips of her fingers, as if to doubt its existence.

Now comes the unmasking of Loys. Note how well the clash is built up. First, Hilarion's denunciation of Loys before Giselle and the assembled villagers. Second, the faltering explanation made by the bewildered Loys to the effect that no harm has been done, for Giselle will merely marry a duke instead of a peasant. Third, Hilarion's crushing rejoinder that Loys is already betrothed to another. Fourth, Hilarion's action in blowing the horn hanging outside the cottage, which action brings the Prince and his daughter upon the scene and reveals to their astonished gaze the tense situation in which the stage is dominated by Duke Albrecht, habited as a peasant. Hilarion's move is like a final and unanswerable check in a grim game of chess. Yet Albrecht, after a moment of embarrassment, recovers his poise, and by his lofty bearing shows that he is the equal of his peers.

This is the prelude to the famous scene of madness which Saint-Georges probably adapted from the " mad scene " in Donizetti's opera, *Lucia di Lammermoor*, founded on the well-known novel, *The Bride of Lammermoor*, by Sir Walter Scott. In the opera, as in the ballet, the heroine loses her reason as the result of disappointed love.

But to return to the action of the ballet. Giselle's acutely sensitive nature cannot withstand so heavy a blow to her fondest hopes. She swoons.[1] On rising, it is clear from her vacant gaze that her mind has given way. She lives in the past, believes herself to be dancing once more with her beloved Loys. This is adroitly conveyed by a repetition of the little *enchaînement* with its characteristic melody : *ballonné—chassé—coupé*, which she first danced with Loys. Suddenly her limbs refuse their office. She resembles a grotesque clockwork toy, the mainspring of which has snapped. In a moment of lucidity her sense of utter frustration passes from the deepest despair to a mad frenzy. She has no longer any desire to live and, snatching up Loys's sword by the point, she forces it into her side. In her last agonies she circles the stage in a mad dance, then stops, makes a few faltering steps and falls to the ground, at the point of death. Her mother supports her in her arms. Loys holds her hand. Hilarion, horrified at the awful consequences of his act, kneels and prays to heaven for forgiveness. The collapse and death of Giselle require careful timing to ensure the maximum dramatic effort. It is a common fault for the dancer to collapse too soon, when the death scene becomes tedious through being too long-drawn out.

This scene of madness followed by Giselle's suicide and death can be deeply moving, but it is not without pitfalls for the *ballerina*. Clearly the dramatic content will vary with the mimetic powers of the dancer taking the rôle of Giselle. But

[1] When Giselle sinks to the ground, her friends and her mother go to her assistance. During this moment of confusion, when Giselle is momentarily masked from the view of the real audience, it is customary for Giselle's mother to let down her daughter's hair in preparation for the next episode, the scene of madness, for dishevelled hair was a conventional stage symbol of a fevered or disordered brain. The effect of sudden illness is sometimes heightened by the mother's carrying a small concealed powder-puff with which during the same moment of confusion, she powders Giselle's cheeks, thus eliminating the blush of real or apparent health.

if the episode is to be presented on a poetic plane, as I submit it must be, then the conception must be lyrical. The state of madness cannot be reproduced with the stark realism of a pathological case ; it can only be hinted at, for the dancer must inspire pity in the beholder, not a sense of repulsion. Again, the dramatic accents must be nicely timed and controlled so that tragedy does not degenerate into crude melodrama. It is a very short step from the sublime to the ridiculous. Passing to a consideration of the *corps de ballet* in this episode, it must be observed that the grouping of the villagers about the dying girl frequently leaves much to be desired, for their attitudes are so perfunctory and so disinterested in relation to the tragedy enacted before their eyes, that one might be led to believe that such scenes were of hourly occurrence.

CHAPTER XIII

HUNTSMEN arrive singly or in small groups, until all are assembled at a prearranged spot. Hilarion enters. He and his companions amuse themselves throwing dice. A nearby church chimes the hour of midnight. The glade takes on a sinister aspect and the huntsmen, seized with fear, seek safety in flight.

Myrtha, Queen of the Wilis, enters at 4, and flashes across back of stage. She re-enters at 3 and travels with *bourrées* to 1, then exits, taking off her veil. She re-enters at 1, walks to centre, makes a *révérence à terre*. *Glissade* to L. with pose in *arabesque à terre*, then slowly raises rear foot to form high *arabesque penchée*, with arm up ; turns in *arabesque*, drops raised leg and makes low *révérence*. Repeats all from *glissade* but to R., ending with *révérence* to 2.

Pas de bourrée to 2, when she turns once on points, then continues *bourrées* to 4, again turns once, then passes from 4—3, when she poses facing 1, L.F. *croisé* and *pointe tendue*, arms *demi-seconde* position.

Series of *temps levés en arabesque* on alternate feet on diagonal 3—1, then faces centre *en attitude*, arms above head. Repeats whole from *temps levés* but to 2, *pas de bourrée* to L., to centre, series of turns on point, arms above head, then sinks on L. knee in deep pose, head looking from under R. arm.

Rises and exits at 8 on first *cadenza* to fetch two branches. Returns with them and runs across stage on second *cadenza*, tossing one branch to R. ; returns, throwing remaining branch to L. Dance concludes with majestic promenade round stage in wide circle to R., taking pose in centre, when Queen summons Wilis.

Veiled Wilis, with arms crossed over their breasts, enter simultaneously from both sides. They advance to centre using 2 slow and 3 quick steps, when they face Queen, who, rising on points, commands them to retire and remove their veils.

Wilis exit and return without veils, when they stand near

the wings in twos and threes, their arms crossed about each other's waists. Queen bids Wilis dance and exits.

Wilis begin with 4 small *révérences*. Now 1st Attendant Wili enters at 1, then 2nd at 2; both stand centre. All Wilis join hands in couples, each pair facing outwards, when each group turns on itself, with *posé* on R. point and *petit batt.* with L.F. Each Wili steps in an *arabesque pliée*, which is held, then repeated 4 times circling about each other. Then all do *bourrées* to centre to form a figure the shape of a star.

All kneel on L. knee facing to centre, arms to floor, backs curved and heads to ground, and do a *port de bras* 4 times, the torso bending backward then forward, the R. arm passing over head.

Wilis rise and form two lines, then travel outwards to wings with a series of *pas de bourrée sur les pointes*. Note that the two Attendants are at head of each line. Towards the end of this step, 1st Attendant runs to 7.

1st Attendant's solo. This concludes with a series of *petits tours* to R. then pose in *arabesque à terre* at 2. Towards the end of this step, 2nd Attendant runs to 7.

2nd Attendant's Solo. This concludes with a series of *petits tours* to L. then pose in *arabesque à terre* at 1.

Ensemble with Wilis doing *chassé—cabriole en arrière en troisième arabesque* followed by *pas de bourrée* to centre, with repeat of whole step outwards to wings.

Queen enters at 3 and executes solo which ends at centre with pose *en troisième arabesque à terre*. She exits at 2 while two Attendants go to centre back; *corps de ballet* do *pas de bourrée* as above.

Two Attendants together execute short dance ending in *petits tours*, one passing to 1, the other to 2.

Ensemble. Wilis are still in two lines. Rear Wilis on each side do a series of *temps levés en arabesque* travelling inwards, returning to original position by means of a sequence of *ballotté* and *jeté en tournant*. This step is repeated 4 times. On the 2nd repeat, the next group down stage join in with same movement. On the 3rd repeat, the next group join in with same movement. On the 4th repeat, the final group nearest stage join in with same movement.

The Wilis now do 8 *temps levés en arabesque* travelling towards the wing opposite to their starting position. That is, the Wilis on the line 1—4, travel to the line 2—3, and *vice versa* ; the group on the right always passes in front of that on the left. Each Wili does a step which ends so that they face inwards. They now cross as before in a series of 15 *temps levés en arabesque*, this time concluding with a *pas de bourrée* on place so that each Wili stands facing outwards.

Queen enters at 3 with *pas de bourrée* and travels with a series of *grand jeté—entrechat six*, first to 1, next to 2 ; then, with a series of *grands jetés en tournant*, she describes a semi-circle to L., ending at 3, followed by a series of *petits tours* to 1. She then does *bourrées* on point in a circle to L., passing to 8—4—7— centre, almost to 5, when she turns on place with *pas de bourrée en tournant*. During this solo the Wilis form three lines parallel to audience and behind Queen, the Attendants standing at either side of her. The whole company do a series of *pas de bourrée* on points, forward and back on place, then *fouetté sauté à l'arabesque* ; this is repeated 4 times in all. Then come 5 *fouettés sautés à l'arabesque*, omitting the *pas de bourrée*. All drop in 5th position and rise on points, arms above head.

After a pause all turn on points to 4, then travel with *pas de bourrée* slowly to centre and sink on one knee, hands crossed before, heads lowered almost to the ground. Still kneeling, all now rise slowly, their bodies bent backward, the L. arm almost on the ground, the R. arm extended upwards above the head.

Still facing 4, all rise from the ground, and, while the Queen exits at 2, the Wilis draw closer to the cross, standing with L.F. in the 4th pos. back, *pointe tendue*. Queen re-enters at 2, bearing a branch of myrtle, during which the Wilis form a line at each side. Queen takes 2 walking steps towards the cross, then, standing in *arabesque à terre*, extends the magic branch over the tomb, when Giselle emerges from her grave, her eyes closed and her arms crossed on her breast, and walks very slowly towards the Queen, who, changing the branch to her L. hand, with her R. hand plucks off Giselle's veil (this occurs on the laſt note of a *cadenza*). As Giselle's face is bared, she opens her eyes. The Queen, ſtepping backwards with 2 slow and 3 quick *pas* to 2, beckons to Giselle, who, facing her, follows, using the same *pas*; Giselle makes a *révérence* to the Queen, wreathing her hands. The Queen sets a ſtar[1] above Giselle's brow, touches her shoulders with the branch and commands her to dance, then exits.

Giselle does 24 quick *temps levés en arabesque* turning to L., then does a *relevé* and *développé en tournant* and runs to 1. She passes from 1—3 with a new *enchaînement* and returns to 1 with a series of *petits tours*, after which she exits. When Giselle begins her dance, the Wilis take up a position *en arabesque*, which is discarded when Giselle runs to 1, but resumed when she exits.

The Queen returns and bids the Wilis leave the glade, then herself exits at 2. (*The ſtage is empty for a brief interval.*)

Enter Albrecht, cloaked and carrying a sheaf of lilies. Heart-broken and in despair, he walks slowly to centre. Looking round, he espies Giselle's grave and goes towards it.

Enter Wilfrid in search of his lord. Seeing the Duke near the grave, he raises his hands in horror.

Albrecht then throws back his cloak and, doffing his cap, hands them both to Wilfrid. Then Albrecht places the lilies on the grave and in utter despair falls to his knees. Wilfrid, fearing for his lord's reason, touches him on the shoulder and implores him to leave the ill-omened glade. Albrecht rises and bids Wilfrid begone. He exits near 3. Albrecht returns close to the grave, and, kneeling facing 5, prays.

Giselle appears from behind the cross and bends towards Albrecht. Conscious of her presence, he looks up, but already she has vanished. He rises, wanders towards centre, seeking the vision. Giselle returns, gliding swiftly on the diagonal 4—2, and, as she passes him, he attempts to catch her as she bounds into the air. She escapes from his grasp and exits at 2. He follows in vain pursuit, then, as he ſtands bewildered, she appears in the diſtance running from 3—4. He turns and sees her juſt as she vanishes at 4. Despondent, Albrecht walks to the centre where, falling on one knee, he prays that the vision may remain with him.

Giselle re-enters at 4, then, looking towards Albrecht, walks

---

[1] According to Gautier's notice of the first performance of *Giselle*, the Queen of the Wilis invested Giselle not with a star, but with a magic garland of asphodel and verbena.

to centre and hovers behind him. Then she goes to 1 and begins to dance in a wide circle about him, moving to her L. in a series of sustained *relevés* and high jumps in which she turns on herself. She then goes to Albrecht, who is still kneeling, and touches his shoulder. He looks up in amazement.

Giselle does 2 small *posés en arabesque* towards 1, her hands cupped a little beyond her chin. Albrecht follows, caressing her wings. As she reaches 1, Albrecht falls on his knees, his hands passing lightly over her skirt as if to assure himself of her existence.

Giselle and Albrecht now dance together : the former from 2 and moving to her R. ; the latter from 4 moving to his L. Note that Albrecht always runs behind Giselle. The step is repeated several times in all, when Giselle exits at 2.

Albrecht, surprised at Giselle's disappearance, searches for her near the grave. But she appears at 2 and runs to 3 to pluck two lilies. Albrecht extends his arms towards her and waits, while Giselle runs to 2, holding a lily in each hand. Giselle and Albrecht again dance together, both passing to their R. This *pas*, based on *ballonné, pas de bourrée* and *grand saut de basque*, is repeated 4 times, crossing on the diagonals. Note that Giselle faces the audience, while Albrecht has his back to it. Albrecht now stands at 4 while Giselle does a series of *glissade chassé— temps levé en arabesque* to 2, then runs to 3 and poses exultantly with arms above head.

Giselle now runs swiftly from 3—1, making a big *jeté en arabesque*, at the same time tossing one of the lilies over her shoulder to Albrecht, who follows in swift pursuit, also springing *en arabesque* and dropping on one knee to pick up the flower, after which he follows her to 3. Giselle now repeats the run and jump on the same diagonal, throwing the second lily and making her exit at 1. Albrecht follows after her as before, but pauses as he picks up the second flower, then exits at 1.

Enter Hilarion at 3, running and looking fearfully over his shoulder. Some Wilis run in at 4 and, standing in *arabesque à terre*, L. arm raised vertically upwards, bar his way. Whichever way Hilarion strives to turn, Wilis successively confront him at 3, 8, 6, 1, and 2, at which last point he is seized by the last arrived group of Wilis. The Queen enters at 2, followed by her two Attendants.

The Wilis, now ranged on the two lines 1—4, 2—3, dance to and from the centre with a *balancé* movement, Hilarion being passed from group to group. All the Wilis, with the exception of the Queen, join hands and, facing outwards, form a giant circle about Hilarion. They make one complete revolution, travelling with small steps, and form into a single line on the diagonal 4—2, standing in *arabesque à terre* and facing 2. As the circle breaks, Hilarion recoils to 4.

Hilarion, espying the Queen, runs along the line of Wilis and falls at her feet, entreating her to spare him, but she coldly refuses. Hilarion retraces his steps along the same diagonal 2—4, in turn approaching each Wili and begging her to spare him. As each ignores his plea, he again approaches the Queen, who tells him that he must die. As he turns away, he is whirled down the line of Wilis. As each Wili pushes him to her companion, she makes a half turn to face 4. When he reaches the end of the line, the last two Wilis make a gesture of seizing him and pushing him into the fatal pool (*actually he exits at* 4). These two Wilis immediately take up their former position at the end of the diagonal.

The Queen, who, facing 4, has watched the death of Hilarion, now, accompanied by her two Attendants, travels with a series of light *jetés* to 8 where she exits. As she is about to leave, the next two Wilis at the head of the line (at 2) exit similarly. As this couple is about to leave, the next pair move up to 2 and exit likewise, and so on until all are gone.

The Queen returns at 4, followed by the Wilis, who run to 2, when, facing that corner, they stand in *arabesque à terre*. While the Wilis remain in this pose, the Queen turns to face 4, her R. arm upraised.

Albrecht runs on at 4 and, kneeling at the Queen's feet, begs for mercy, which is refused. Giselle, also entering at 4, hurries to place herself in front of Albrecht, and adds her entreaties that the Queen may spare her lover. When she again refuses, Giselle urges Albrecht to hasten to the sanctuary of the cross. The Queen at once signs to the Wilis to intercept him. Shielding their eyes against the radiance from the cross, they run in a circle from 2—1—8—4; the first half aligning on the diagonal 4—2, the second half forming a line parallel to and behind them, all stand in *arabesque à terre* position facing 2.

Despite the efforts of the Wilis, Albrecht reaches the cross, where he is joined by Giselle, who extends her arms to shield him. The Queen follows but stops near the cross, halted by its protecting influence. Standing in *arabesque à terre*, she opposes the power of her myrtle branch, which suddenly snaps in her hand. The Queen recoils in fear, while the

Wilis turn their heads away and cover their eyes with up-raised arm.

Giselle and Albrecht breathe a sigh of relief, but the Queen, inexorable in her hate, again approaches the cross and commands Giselle to dance; the Wilis lift their heads. Now the Queen slowly retraces her steps, beckoning to Giselle, who follows her as if in a trance. Meanwhile the Wilis slowly form into two lines near the wings, from 1—4, and from 2—3. Albrecht remains beside the cross.

Adage : Giselle

Giselle begins with a *développé à la seconde*, then *fouetté à l'arabesque*, turning in the same pose from 1—2, then *assemblé—entrechat six—dégagé* with a low *révérence*. She now raises working leg to *arabesque penchée* and holds this position. Rising, she goes to Wilis on line 2—3 and implores their help, while Albrecht makes a similar entreaty to the Wilis on the line 1—4. The Wilis make a *port de bras* expressive of refusal. Giselle and Albrecht cross to opposite sides, when the same actions of entreaty and refusal are repeated. Giselle and Albrecht pass to centre.

Adage : Giselle & Albrecht

Giselle, supported by Albrecht, does a *développé à la quatrième devant croisé*, followed by a *grand rond de jambe à l'arabesque*, turning to face 1. He then sways her from side to side and turns her to R. until she faces 1, when she does a *développé à la quatrième devant* to 1.

Giselle, now dancing alone, drops on to R.F. and does *pas de bourrée* followed by *grand jeté en tournant*, then, slowly turning on points, she goes towards Albrecht, who catches her L. wrist, when she does a *développé écarté* to 3, leaning to 1 ; this *développé* is repeated.

Two Wilis at head of line 2—3 draw Giselle gently away from Albrecht, while the two Wilis at head of opposite line draw away Albrecht. But the lovers elude their captors and return to centre ; Albrecht facing 1, Giselle opposite 3.

Giselle, holding Albrecht's R. hand, does a *développé à la quatrième devant* to 3. Releasing his hand, she half-turns sharply

to 1, so that her raised leg is now *en arabesque,* Albrecht supporting her at the waist. Now he sways her from side to side, then
turns her to R. until she faces 1, at the end of which she does a
développé à la quatrième devant to 1.

Giselle leaps upward, taking an *arabesque* position, when
Albrecht catches her and holds her at shoulder level in this pose.
He gently lowers her to the ground when she does a series
of *pas de bourrée* in a circle to her L. to 3, returning centre, when
he drops on his R. knee, facing 1. Giselle comes behind him
and, placing her L. hand on his L. shoulder, raises her rear
leg *en arabesque,* her R. arm forming half 5th pos. *en haut.*

The Queen goes towards the lovers. Giselle rises and bows
to her, Albrecht goes to 3. The Queen commands Giselle to
dance again, then goes to 2. Giselle faces 5, with R.F. in 4th
pos. back, *pointe tendue,* arms crossed in front.

Solo : Giselle

Giselle does *glissade sauté—double rond de jambe en dehors* with
R.F., the raised leg falling low, the body and R. arm moving
in co-ordination and to same side. This movement is repeated
to alternate sides 4 times in all and travelling back. She now
does series of *soubresauts* travelling to 1, arms raised *en arabesque,*
then *sissonne* and *pas de bourrée,* finishing at 1, with same pose
as at beginning.

Solo : Albrecht

Albrecht travels from 3—1 with step consisting of *pas de basque
—chassé—temps levé en arabesque—jeté en attitude—assemblé—
3 entrechats six.* This *enchaînement* is repeated with a change
in the last 2 *entrechats six.* He now travels to centre with
entrechat cinq—posé—assemblé—sissonne à l'arabesque. He then
does a *développé à la seconde—retiré—2 tours en arabesque en dedans,*
and runs to 2, where he waits for Giselle, who runs from 1.

Travelling from 2—centre Giselle does a *développé à la
quatrième devant* with R.F., then, jumping off L.F., is lifted
vertically into the air by Albrecht, who lowers her to the ground
on her R.F. This movement is repeated 4 times in all, the lifts
being gradually taken higher and higher. Arrived at centre,
Albrecht lifts Giselle 4 times in *arabesque* position to alternate

sides (to 8, 6, 8, 6) then once to 5, when Giselle does a *développé* to 4th pos. front, after which she runs to 5 to begin her solo.

Solo : Giselle

Giselle travels backward on the line 5 to centre, doing *entrechat quatre—relevé passé derrière* on alternate feet, then 4 *relevés passés derrière* on alternate feet, arms 5th *en bas*. This step is repeated then followed by 16 *entrechats quatre* travelling from centre to 3, gradually raising arms *en arabesque*. She then goes from 3—1 with a series of light turns, concluding with a *pas de chat*, which brings her facing 5.

Solo : Albrecht

Albrecht travels from 3—1 doing *glissade—double cabriole—2 jetés en attitude—assemblé—3 entrechats six*, which *enchaînement* is repeated with slight alteration at end. Then follows *ballotté devant—ballotté derrière—2 chassé, coupé, jeté en tournant*, ending in *attitude* position, the raised foot being passed through ready to begin again from *ballotté*, with two repeats of this *enchaînement*.

He beseeches the Wilis to spare him from dancing further, but they refuse, whereupon he goes to 3 and faces 1. Travelling from 3—1, he does series of *temps levés—chassé—assemblé—tour en l'air*, then series of *pirouettes en dehors* followed by a *double tour en l'air*, ending with his falling full length to the ground.

Giselle enters at 4 and, with a gesture of endearment, goes to Albrecht and tries to help him to rise. Failing in this, she goes to the Queen at 2, stands for an instant in an attitude of supplication, then begins to dance.

Solo : Giselle

Giselle travels from 2—4, doing *temps levé—chassé—fouette à l'arabesque* facing 2, then *pas de bourrée* to 4, then *fouetté en tournant à l'arabesque* facing 2, this is repeated to 2 and then to 4, when she returns to centre. She then does *entrechat quatre —relevé—rond de jambe en dehors*, this sequence is repeated to opposite side, then follow 3 *retirés*, the last being held.

She now goes to Albrecht, still lying prostrate, and hovers

behind him. Travelling to 3 with a series of *posés*, she makes a beckoning movement of her R. wrist to Albrecht, who painfully rises and staggers to 3, behind Giselle. Now she travels to 1 with a series of small *jetés derrière*, making fluttering movements of her wrists, then runs off at 1, followed by Albrecht. The Wilis remain motionless.

They are still ranged on the lines 1—4, and 2—3, one Attendant at the head of each line, with the Queen at 2. Now they all face inwards and do *temps levé en arabesque—2 ballottés —saut de basque—pas de chat*. This *enchaînement* is repeated 4 times in all. They now do *pas de bourrée* towards centre, almost meeting, then, doing *pas de bourrée* in reverse direction, they return to their previous two lines 1—4 and 2—3.

Albrecht enters at 4 and, facing 4, travels from 4—2 with *pas de bourrée—grand jeté battu en tournant—assemblé—sissonne battu en avant*. This *enchaînement* is done 3 times in all, when he again flings himself before the Queen and begs for mercy.

His appeal dismissed, he struggles to his feet and travels in a circle to his R. with a series of *chassé—temps levé en arabesque*, then staggers to 3, at which juncture Giselle enters. As he lightly supports her about the waist, she travels on the line 3—8 in a series of 5 *temps levés en arabesque*, followed by *assemblé*, after which he lifts her *en arabesque* in the air, then lowers her to face 2, when the whole is repeated from 8 to below 6, then from below 6 to 1. Giselle then does 3 small *temps levés en arabesque* to 2, facing 2, while Albrecht staggers to 4, back to audience.

Giselle travels from 2—4 with *ballonné—pas de bourrée—grand saut de basque*; Albrecht does the same from 4—2. This *enchaînement* is repeated 4 times in all to alternate sides, at the end of which the lovers are at centre. During this last *enchaînement*, Wilis do same step as at beginning of Coda, but twice only and in one straight line on each side.

Giselle and Albrecht do *fouetté sauté à l'arabesque* 6 times to alternate sides, when Albrecht falls exhausted on his knees, while Giselle stands behind him on points, arms 5th *en haut*. During this, the Wilis do 6 *ballonnés* on place, turn on points, then drop inside foot to 4th pos. back, *pointe tendue*, bringing arms to *demi-seconde* pos.

Giselle goes to the Queen and again entreats her to spare Albrecht. When she coldly refuses, Giselle goes down the line of Wilis imploring their help, each in turn, which they decline with a *port de bras* of negation. She returns to the Queen and resumes her entreaty, during which Albrecht rises and goes towards Wilis on L. side, but, at a peremptory gesture from the Queen, they force him to dance again in their midst.

Now the Wilis do *temps levés* to centre and then travel to wings with a series of *pas de bourrée* to form a line on each side.

Meanwhile Albrecht, in centre, does a series of *temps de poisson* and again falls on his knees, then sinks to the ground. Giselle remains by the Queen still beseeching her to spare Albrecht.

But now the first rays of dawn invade the dark glade and Giselle realises that the power of the Wilis is quickly drawing to an end. A distant bell strikes the hour of four. Immediately all the Wilis, the Queen last, go slowly towards the cross, forming into three lines on the diagonal 4—2 and facing 4, where they stand in usual *pointe tendue* position, arms slowly raised to 5th *en haut*. Then they sink on their left knee and, bowing their heads over their knee to the ground, repeat same *port de bras* as at end of invocation previous to Giselle's first entrance from the tomb. Meanwhile Giselle, kneeling behind Albrecht, tenderly supports his head on her knee. The Wilis rise on points and form in two lines from 1—4, and 2—3, with an Attendant at the head of each line, then, with *pas de bourrée*, exit into nearest wing, the Queen being the last to leave at 2.

As the Wilis leave, Albrecht struggles slowly to his feet, Giselle supporting his outstretched arms. Giselle backs slowly to centre, while Albrecht tries to prevent her from returning to her grave. But he fails and she vanishes behind the cross. Albrecht, distraught, summons all his strength to follow her but, exhausted, falls in a swoon at the foot of the cross.

The curtain slowly falls.

CHAPTER XIV

THE second act opens on a darkened stage. Some huntsmen are seen strolling in little groups through the forest. They are followed by Hilarion. Why huntsmen should range the forest at close on midnight is not clear. Some producers have tried to answer this riddle by making them sit down and throw dice, during which a sudden storm springs up and causes them to take flight. Hilarion, catching sight of the cross with Giselle's name upon it, is seized with fear and hurries into the depths of the wood.

From the trees comes Myrtha, Queen of the Wilis. Her dance, its direction, and her sweeping gestures are really a kind of incantation, a consecration of the mystic grove to the unholy rites shortly to take place. The rites at an end, she selects a sprig of rosemary[1] for sceptre and summons her subjects, who emerge from the shadows. The Wilis are clad in white ballet dresses, which symbolise their ethereal quality, and wear short bridal veils. As a general rule the Wilis emerge from the trees simultaneously, with almost military precision. But Gautier imagined the Wilis arriving from all parts of the world so that it would be more logical if they alighted in succession, like birds flying to a common meeting-place. Moreover, Gautier wished the Wilis to bear some token indicative of the respective lands from which they came, which was to be further expressed in their manner of dancing. Whether this was ever achieved in the original production it is difficult to say.

The assembly complete, Myrtha informs her subjects that they are to admit a new sister to their number. Now follows a group dance of initiation in which the dancers should try and convey the impression that they are intangible spirits, wisps of wreathing mist. The dance ends in an unusual manner with the Wilis having their backs to the

---

[1] There is an element of symbolism in this choice, for, in classic times, rosemary—for remembrance—was worn at both bridals and burials. Moreover, lovers who, through unhappiness, died at an early age, had garlands of rosemary placed on their biers.

audience as they are massed on a diagonal line towards Giselle's grave. They take up a new position as Myrtha, extending her sceptre, causes Giselle to emerge from the earthy confines of her grave.

This is one of the first problems for the producer. How is Giselle to make her entrance? It would seem that in the original production, the willow branches lifted, the mound parted, and Giselle, attired in her white ballet dress, and covered with a shroud-like veil, came slowly into view, borne upwards through a trap. But not every stage contains such machinery, hence it is often necessary to devise other forms of entry.

The most usual is for Giselle to issue from behind the shelter of the cross, but this manner of entry is inclined to be too casual. Actually, Giselle is a corpse[1] which Myrtha, by means of the supernatural powers with which she has been invested, endows with fleeting life. Therefore one would expect Giselle's first entrance to be almost mechanical, slow and faltering like those of a hypnotised person. When the veil is drawn from her face, her eyes would open slowly as from a heavy sleep ; she would gaze wonderingly at her strange surroundings, her arms still crossed over her breast. Seeing Myrtha, she instinctively inclines her head in homage. Myrtha places the star of the Wilis on her forehead and with a wave of her branch causes little wings to spring from her shoulders. This last is a charming mechanical device which, long since omitted, might well be restored. Then, as Giselle feels life once more pulsating in her icy veins, she expresses her joy in a bewildering succession of turns, here used to express ecstasy. Later the Wilis and their new sister leave the glade and the stage is empty.

Enter Albrecht, attended by his squire, Wilfrid. The Duke, dressed in dark clothes and wrapped in a long cloak, walks slowly and sadly in search of Giselle. He carries flowers to place on her grave. Arrived before it, he turns to his squire and bids him withdraw, as he wishes to be alone with his thoughts. Then he doffs his cap and cloak and, placing the flowers on the grave, kneels in prayer. Frequently this uncloaking is made an excuse for a vulgar theatrical effect, for the cloak, thrown back with a flamboyant gesture, proves to be lined with a startling shade of mauve, at the same time the Duke is seen to be wearing hose of a similar vivid hue. It is curious, too, how Albrecht

---

[1] In this act, Spessivtzeva made up her features all white, into which she worked a touch of blue.

generally carries a great armful of white lilies, which I find singularly inappropriate and displeasing, for they suggest a previous visit to a florist. It is quite possible that these two pieces of "business" are traditional, but surely they are a complete negation of what one conceives to be Albrecht's character. The lilies suggest the kind of artificiality which one feels sure he would abhor. Knowing Giselle's modest tastes and love of simple things, is it not far more likely that he would choose a posy of wild flowers gathered by himself in the woods she loved?

The prayer scene varies considerably in interpretation, according to the dancer concerned. Lifar, for instance, gives an impassioned rendering of grief, flinging himself upon the grave and even repeatedly striking his head against the ground in a frenzy of despair. But the spectator is embarrassed rather than moved by such emotional outbursts. Genuine heartfelt grief is too crushing for display and finds expression in such small intimate actions as the slow bending of the head, the clasping and unclasping of the hands, or the furtive brushing away of a tear.

While Albrecht kneels in prayer he is startled by a phantom form which he recognises to be his beloved Giselle. This leads to a charming *pas de deux* in which they seem to relive those bygone happy hours. The most beautiful moment in their dance is when Giselle, taking a flower in each hand, crosses the stage in a series of high bounds on a diagonal line from back to front, casting a flower behind her as she does so, which Albrecht, following in pursuit, tries to catch. What kind of flower should Giselle use? Some dancers hold a lily in each hand, an unwise choice because a long-stemmed flower tends to make the dancer's arms appear almost as long as her legs. On the other hand, if the flower be too small, it cannot be seen. Markova solved this problem by using a small silver flower with silver leaves, which, glittering in the light, was easily visible.

Once again the stage is empty and Hilarion is seen returning. To his horror he finds himself back in the dreaded glade. But before he can flee he is hemmed in by a roving band of Wilis. They are joined by others. Vainly he tries to escape only to be forced to accompany them in their mad dance. The melody here has an unusually dynamic quality, a remorseless driving rhythm which should be reflected in the movements of the Wilis and their victim.

The Wilis then change their formation and take up a diagonal line with Myrtha at the end nearest the footlights. Hilarion, fearing for his life, kneels for mercy, but is contemptuously dismissed. Then he is tossed cruelly from one Wili to the other. As he reaches the end of the line, I always feel that the Wilis should burst upon him like a mighty wave and dash him into the pool. Above the misty forms would momentarily be seen his wildly waving arms, then they would vanish and all would be over. In *Les Beautés de l'Opéra* there is a woodcut illustrating this incident, which suggests a similar treatment in the original production. In contemporary versions the more usual impression is that Hilarion has committed suicide, for he half rolls, half staggers down the line and then leaps into obscurity.

Now some observations on the manner in which the Wilis kill their victim. They do not induce Hilarion to dance so that he dies from exhaustion. That is only the means to an end. They cause their victim to dance so that he may become subservient to their will, then he is drawn towards the pool into which he falls and is drowned.

Do you remember the air to which the Wilis dance after they have disposed of Hilarion ? It has a curious half-triumphant, half-mocking quality which is seldom found in the dancers' movements.

When the Wilis have left the glade in search of other victims, Albrecht and Giselle return. It is not long before they are discovered by some of the Wilis. Giselle, alarmed for her lover's safety, bids him stand in the shadow of the cross, which is a sure sanctuary. She begs Myrtha to spare her lover, but the Queen is unforgiving and remorseless. Indeed, she selects the cruellest of all weapons in the feminine armoury. She will play on Albrecht's love for Giselle in order to lure him from the protection of the cross, when, once within her magic circle, she can destroy his will and drive him into the deadly pool.

She commands Giselle to dance and to put forth her most seductive movements. This is the most difficult scene for the *ballerina*, for she must try to suggest on the one hand that she is the slave of the Queen's will, while, on the other, she must contrive to keep Albrecht close to the cross. But the torture of being separated from his beloved is too much for Albrecht. He leaves his sanctuary, bounds towards Giselle, and shares in her dances. Gradually, as he is forced to traverse the fatal circle, he feels himself seized with a strange weakness; he is forced to pause for breath; he staggers, falls, struggles to his feet and tries to dance again. This *pas de deux* is the most difficult scene in which to achieve conviction. It can be most touching and inspiring, and it can be, and often is, ludicrous.

In this act there is a flaw in the choreographic structure— Albrecht's *pas seul*. Although it has the elevation so characteristic of Perrot's choreography, I venture to doubt whether this *variation* was part of the original production. Technically of great difficulty, it is merely a *tour de force*, and to my mind quite alien to the admirably composed and highly expressive choreography of the long *pas de deux* between Giselle and Albrecht. The latter's *pas seul* does not spring from the body of the work like the other dances; it seems to be imposed upon it, and has the effect of a false note in an otherwise beautiful melody.

We now come to the final episode, when Albrecht is preserved from harm by the coming of the dawn, which causes the Wilis to melt away like the morning mist before the sun. There is a brief parting between the lovers and Giselle returns to the cold earth whence she came. But how should this be effected? Does she return to her grave? This would seem to be the most logical conclusion, but contemporary accounts of the ballet state that Giselle, already feeling her strength ebbing, sinks to the ground, when flowers spring up and cover her from sight as she sinks beneath the earth. That this was the original rendering is born out by contemporary illustrations of this episode.[1] Albrecht bounds forward, but too late. He plucks a rose from this sacred spot and presses it to his lips. At this point Wilfrid and Bathilde enter in search of Albrecht. They come forward and support him just as he falls back overcome with grief and emotion.

But this ending has long since been changed. In contemporary productions Giselle disappears into the shadow of the cross, when Albrecht staggers and falls heavily to the ground—presumably dead. But if this be true, then Giselle's devices to save

---

[1] According to the authors' original intention, Giselle was to return to her grave. But Adolphe Adam reveals in his unpublished *Mémoires* (quoted Pougin, *op. cit*, p. 162) that *he* was responsible for the changed ending. "At the dress rehearsal I made an alteration which was approved by my collaborators, Saint-Georges and Théophile Gautier. Giselle, at the first rays of dawn, re-entered her tomb. I did not consider this ending sufficiently poetic. I had the idea of making her lover deposit her in a bank of flowers and of making her gradually disappear. This climax made a better ending to this very poetic legend and achieved all the anticipated success."

Albrecht, which she has planned with such loving care, have all been in vain and would give the victory to the Wilis, which we know is not the case. It is argued, however, that the death of Albrecht affords a more dramatic finale. Even if this be conceded, I must maintain that such an ending is inconclusive, for what happens to Bathilde ? It will be her ambition, and it is a noble and generous one, to fill the place of Giselle.

CHAPTER XV

GISELLE, first performed at the Opera, Paris, in 1841, remained in the repertory of the national theatre until 1849, the title-rôle being always danced by Carlotta Grisi. It was revived in 1852, with Mlle. Guérinot, and in 1853—although only two performances were given—with Regina Forli. From 1841 to 1853 the rôle of Albrecht was taken by Lucien Petipa. *Giselle* was then dropped from the repertory until 1863, when it was revived for the Paris *début* of the Russian *ballerina*, Martha Muravieva. The ballet continued to be regularly performed until 1868, when it was again withdrawn from the repertory. It is of interest to mention that the season of 1866 was marked by the Paris *début* of Adela Grantzova, a product of the Imperial Russian Ballet, although of German origin. More than fifty years elapsed before the ballet was again revived, in 1924, for the Paris *début* of Olga Spessivtzeva, the role of Albrecht being taken first by Albert Aveline and later by Gaston Ricaux. The next revival was in 1932, again with Spessivtzeva in the title-rôle, but with the part of Albrecht interpreted for the first time by Serge Lifar. This production was revived in 1938 with new settings and costumes by Leyritz, and no doubt this is the version presented to-day.

The fame of *Giselle* quickly reached England, where it was soon introduced to London audiences. But, curiously enough, it was not the ballet which was presented, but a drama in 2 acts and 8 scenes called *Giselle or The Phantom Night Dancers*, written by William Moncrieff, and based on the ballet he had seen at Paris. This concoction is described as " A Dramatic, Melo-dramatic, Choreographic, Fantastique [*sic*], Traditionary Tale of Superstition," and was first performed at the Theatre Royal, Sadler's Wells, on August 23rd, 1841. *Giselle* also inspired the opera, *The Night Dancers*, which once enjoyed considerable popularity in England. The libretto was by George Soane and the music by Edward James Loder. This opera was first performed at the Princess's Theatre, Oxford Street, on October 28th, 1846.

The actual ballet was first produced in London on March 12th,

1842, at Her Majesty's Theatre, the principal rôles being taken by Carlotta Grisi and Jules Perrot, while the Myrtha was Louise Fleury; but the choreography would appear to have undergone some revision since it is ascribed to Deshayes and Perrot. The ballet repeated its Paris triumph. The year following there was a revival of *Giselle* at the Princess's Theatre, London, on October 9th, when the ballet provided the pendant to a varied programme consisting of an Italian opera, followed by a dramatic piece. *The Times*[1], while affording little information about the ballet proper, declares it to have been " very beautifully put on the stage, and . . . the groupings . . . excellently managed. Gilbert and Miss Ballin were the Duke and Giselle, and danced to the loudest applause." I do not know who was responsible for the choreography or what relation it bore to the original Coralli-Perrot production. George Gilbert and Miss Ballin, who were husband and wife, had danced for many years with increasing success at Drury Lane and other London theatres. They are among the best English dancers[2] of the Romantic Ballet in England. Apart from Miss Ballin, I have been unable to discover throughout the nineteenth century any other English *danseuse* who achieved success in the title-rôle of Giselle. It is of interest, however, to record that the ballet was revived at the Empire Theatre, on December 26th, 1884, with Alice Holt as Giselle and Mlle. Sismondi as Loys. The ballet was preceded by *Pocohontas*, an operetta by Grundy and Solomon.

It will be noticed that the rôle of Loys was danced *en travestie*, that is, by a woman dressed as a man. The production had a lukewarm reception, and it would appear that the miming left something to be desired, for *The Times* critic observes " Pantomimic action is an all but extinct art in England and it would not have been easy last night to comprehend the story without the aid of a few analytical remarks explaining the love of Hilarion, the adventures of Loys, a disguised prince, and the nature of the Wilis, or dancing fairies " (December 27th).

The most important London performance of *Giselle* since 1842 was that presented by the Diaghilev Ballet on October 16th, 1911, at the Royal Opera, Covent Garden, with Karsavina and Nijinsky. Then came the production of the Pavlova Company in 1913, with Anna Pavlova in the title-rôle. The first presentation by an all-English company was that of the Vic-Wells

---

[1] October 10th, 1843.

[2] For an account of the Gilberts, see *Dance Index*, Sept.–Dec. 1943, which contains *The Romantic Ballet in England*, by G. Chaffee.

Ballet at the "Old Vic" on January 1st, 1934, the choreography being revived by Nicholas Sergeyev. This production was dominated by a remarkable performance of the title-rôle by a young English dancer, Alicia Markova, who achieved a striking success, especially in the second act. Her technical brilliance, featherweight lightness, and moving interpretation did much to popularise this ballet with English audiences. After Markova left the company in 1935, the rôle of Giselle was given in January, 1937, to Margot Fonteyn, whose performance has many attractive features, although she lacks the rare elevation and phantom-like quality essential to the second act.

Giselle was revived by the Markova-Dolin Company (1935), the Ballet Guild (1941), and the International Ballet (1942). It is a striking testimony to the ballet's popularity that at one time in 1942 it was being given in London by three different companies. The centenary of *Giselle* was celebrated in England by the Ballet Guild on June 28th, 1941, with a performance of the ballet at the Rudolf Steiner Hall, London, the title-rôle being taken by Hélène Wolska, a young dancer possessed of an unusual elevation and rare lightness ; she is of English extraction, despite her assumed Polish surname. The production was by Molly Lake, who also danced with appropriate dignity the rôle of Myrtha.

Giselle was first performed in Russia on December 18th, 1842, at the Bolshoy Theatre, St. Petersburg, with Elena Andreyanova. The choreography, however, was a suggestion rather than a reproduction of the original work. Andreyanova, an excellent dancer who performed many of the rôles associated with Taglioni, when the *ballerina* had returned to Europe, was much favoured by Gedeonov, the director of the Imperial Theatres. Desiring her to achieve success in a quite new ballet freed of all memories of Taglioni, in 1841 he sent his *maître de ballet*, Titus, to Paris, to find a suitable work for Andreyanova. Titus reached the French capital in June and thus saw *Giselle*, which pleased him so much that he wished to reproduce it immediately at St. Petersburg. But, instead of commissioning Coralli or Perrot to produce the ballet for him, he relied on his memory.

In January, 1843, Lucile Grahn visited St. Petersburg and made her début in *Giselle*, achieving a triumph in the second act. But she had made only two appearances when she was taken ill and her further performances were cancelled. In 1848 Fanny Elssler arrived at St. Petersburg, where she made her *début* on October 10th, again in *Giselle*. Two years later she was followed by Carlotta Grisi herself, who made her first Russian appearance as Giselle at St. Petersburg on October 8th. On February 2nd, 1856, Nadezhda Bogdanova, a Russian dancer of rare promise, made her *début* in *Giselle*. From then onwards numerous Russian dancers sought to win their spurs by making their *début* in the famous rôle, for instance, Muravieva (1863), Kemmerer (1866), Gorshenkova (1875), Vazem (1878)—but there is no need to prolong the list. Russia has a particular importance in relation to *Giselle*, for it is the one country where the ballet has remained constantly in the repertory of the State Theatres, having been continually performed since its first production there in 1842, both during the Imperial *régime* and now under the Soviet Government.

In Italy, *Giselle* was first performed at the Teatro alla Scala, Milan, on January 17th, 1843, but with new music by N. Bajetti and new choreography by A. Cortesi. It is possible, however, that there may have been earlier performances at some of the provincial theatres.

In America, New York had its first sight of *Giselle* at the Park Theatre, on February 2nd, 1846, the title-rôle being taken by Mme. Augusta, a French dancer who became very popular with American audiences. The first American production was given at the Howard Athenæum, Boston, on January 1st, 1846, the chief rôles being taken by two Philadelphians, Mary Ann Lee[1], the first American *première danseuse* of note, and George W. Smith, the first American *premier danseur noble*. Mary Lee, who had previously made many tours with various companies, decided to improve her technique by taking a course of study in Paris, where she arrived in 1844. There she studied for nearly a year under Jean Coralli, and when she returned to America towards the end of 1845 she brought with her the choreographic scores of *Giselle*, *La Fille du Danube*, and *La Jolie Fille de Gand*. The most recent productions in America were that of the Mordkin Ballet (1937) at the Majestic Theatre, New York, with Lucia Chase in the title-rôle, and that devised by Anton Dolin for the Ballet Theatre (1940) with Annabelle Lyon and Patricia Bowman alternately as Giselle and himself as Albrecht. In 1941 Markova joined the Ballet Theatre and again gave her famous interpretation of the title-rôle of *Giselle*.

The framework of *Giselle* has undergone many changes during its long history. The original musical score has been

---

[1] For an account of this dancer, see *Dance Index*, May, 1943, which contains *Mary Ann Lee : First American Giselle*, by Lillian Moore.

altered by omitting some numbers and reducing the length of others, while in some versions music from other works has been interpolated. The choreographic structure has been similarly changed. Finally, the scenes themselves have been subjected to alteration and cuts.

It may be of interest to examine the principal changes in the sequence of scenes in the ballet as it is performed to-day, in relation to the original synopsis. Most, if not all, contemporary English productions are the work of Nicholas Sergeyev, formerly *régisseur* at the Maryinsky Theatre, St. Petersburg, and are probably based on the ballet as performed there from 1884–1887, during which years Marius Petipa finally revised the standardised version, which Perrot produced at St. Petersburg in 1851, and which he himself subjected to many modifications during his service in the Imperial Russian Ballet.

ACT ONE

1. According to the original scenario, after Hilarion has made his first entrance, Albrecht, disguised as a peasant, emerges from his hut attended by Wilfrid, whom he dismisses. The squire bows low before departing, an act of homage which arouses Hilarion's suspicions regarding his peasant rival. In many contemporary versions, we first see Albrecht, richly dressed, and Wilfrid approaching the hut, which they enter. Then follows the scene above. This alteration is a decided improvement, for the change of costume is clearly seen.

2. The hunting-party is now comparatively small in numbers. Originally, apart from the Prince of Courland and his daughter, there were 8 lords, 8 ladies, and 4 pages.

3. The scene where Bathilde, having conferred a gold chain on Giselle, asks her if she is in love, and Giselle replies in the affirmative, pointing to Loys's hut as the abode of her lover, is no longer played. Neither does Bathilde express a wish to see Giselle's *fiancé*, nor inform her that she, too, is betrothed.

4. The return from the vintage, once an imposing spectacle, with its decorated wagon and trophy in the form of Bacchus sitting astride a cask, now consists only of the peasant girls and youths. In the original production there were 16 of each, plus 8 *coryphées*, augmented by 24 children (18 girls and 6 boys) and 4 musicians.

5. The crowning of Giselle as Queen of the Vintage is frequently omitted.

6. The scene of madness now resembles a phrase of mime set to music and varied with a little dancing, instead of being largely danced as it was when first produced, to judge by contemporary notices. I also have very vivid memories of Pavlova in this episode, whose dancing expressed delirium and culminated in a series of frenzied *petits tours* ending with her collapse and death.

7. The scene at the end of the first act where Albrecht, having discovered that Giselle is dead, seizes his sword to kill himself, has been altered. Instead, Albrecht snatches up the sword with the intention of cutting down Hilarion. Again, in the final scene just before the curtain falls, Albrecht, crazed with grief, is not led away by his friends ; he now kneels sadly beside the dead body of his beloved.

ACT TWO

1. The scene of the huntsmen playing dice is frequently omitted.

2. In the original production, after Myrtha's first entrance, Perrot employed many effects of Wilis flying through the air, emerging from clumps of reeds, or darting from flower to flower. These effects were produced by mechanical devices of his own invention, an ingenious system of wires and counterpoises. Such effects[1] have long since fallen into disuse.

3. The scene in which a party of village youths, led by an old peasant, cross the enchanted glade and narrowly escape the fascinations of the Wilis, is no longer played.

4. In the scene where Albrecht, accompanied by Wilfrid, enters the glade in search of Giselle's tomb, the Duke is no longer presented as a man crazed with fear and with his clothes awry. He is outwardly calm and dignified, although oppressed with grief.

5. In the scene where Hilarion is captured by the Wilis and lured to his death by drowning in the pool, Albrecht is no longer a concealed witness of that tragic event. He exits with Giselle after the famous dance in which she bounds across the glade on a diagonal line, throwing a flower to her lover as she does so.

[1] In the 1946 revival of *Giselle* by the Sadler's Wells Ballet at the Royal Opera, Covent Garden, the episode of the " flying " Wilis was restored, but the effect was not entirely satisfactory.

6. The rôle of Hilarion, which apparently contained a measure of dancing, has now become a purely mimed rôle.

* *

*

The study of a classic drama instinctively revives memories of famous players associated with it. So it is with *Giselle*. The list of Albrechts is extensive and varied, for instance, Lucien Petipa, Jules Perrot, Louis Mérante, Pavel Gerdt, Vaslav Nijinsky, Pierre Vladimirov, Anatol Obukhov, Albert Aveline, Gaston Ricaux, Anton Dolin, Serge Lifar, Robert Helpmann, Harold Turner, Igor Youskevich. Among the most celebrated portraits are those of Lucien Petipa, Jules Perrot, and, in more recent times, those of Vaslav Nijinsky (1910), Anton Dolin (1932), Serge Lifar (1932) and Anatol Obukhov. It is one of the very few conceptions of Nijinsky which I have missed, but Alexandre Benois, who is familiar with his rendering, declares, " He made the grief of the repentant seducer profoundly pathetic ; the scene where the Wilis, exalted by Hilarion's doom, try to drag him, too, to his death became genuinely terrifying." Again, referring to Nijinsky's first entrance in Act II, he observes, " Only a genius could have given so authentic an image of the youth pining for his dead beloved."[1]

Of the many Albrechts I have seen I should place Dolin first. He is an excellent partner and possessed of the exceptional technique which the rôle demands. He moves with grace and dignity and invests the mimed scenes with an engaging tenderness and sincerity, and shows a delicate appreciation of the varied situations. Finally, he creates the romantic mood which is an integral part of the ballet. Lifar's interpretation, while full of interest and technically exciting, suffers from an unfortunate tendency towards over-emphasis in the dramatic scenes. In short, he over-plays the part so that it not only becomes equal in importance to that of Giselle, but even overshadows it, thus disturbing the dramatic balance of the piece.

I have seen only one Myrtha that has fulfilled my conception of the rôle, the interpretation of Alexandra Danilova. Of earlier exponents, the performance of Adèle Dumilâtre, the creator of the rôle, and that of Louise Fleury, have been highly praised by contemporaries. Among recent portraits those of the American dancer, Rosella Hightower, and of the English dancer, Joyce Græme, have been commended.

[1] *Op. cit.*, pp. 71 and 290.

The names of those dancers who have essayed the title-rôle must be legion. Here is a list of some of the best-known interpretations of Giselle : Carlotta Grisi (1841), Elena Andreyanova (1842), Lucile Grahn (1843), Fanny Cerito (1843), Marie Taglioni (1843), Mary Lee (1846), Fanny Elssler (1848), Nadezhda Bogdanova (1856), Amalia Ferraris (1859), Carolina Rosati (1862), Martha Muravieva (1862), Adela Grantzova (1866), Zina Mérante (1867), Ekaterina Vazem (1878), I. Gorshenkova (1884), Emma Bessone (1887), Grimaldi (1899), Olga Preobrazhenskaya (1899), Carlotta Zambelli (1901), Anna Pavlova (1903), Thamar Karsavina (1910), Olga Spessivtzeva (1924), Alicia Markova (1934), Vera Nemtchinova (1935,) Margot Fonteyn (1937), Tamara Toumanova (1938), Alexandra Danilova (1943), Galina Ulanova (1944), and Sally Gilmour (1945). To these names I must add those of Yvette Chauviré and Alicia Alonso, as I am uncertain as to the precise year in which they made their first appearance in the rôle.

But of these how many could be classed as outstanding performances ? Among dancers of the nineteenth century, the rendering of Grisi certainly, and perhaps those of Grahn and Ferraris. Among dancers within living memory, the interpretations of Karsavina and Danilova have been rated highly, and I can record that the performances of Pavlova, Spessivtzeva, and Markova moved me deeply.

I can still visualise the elegiac quality of Pavlova's interpretation, her miming in the scene of madness being so moving that it not only deeply affected the audience, but also the members of her company, who could not restrain their tears. Of all the many ballets Pavlova danced, *Giselle* was undoubtedly the one she loved the most, and so intensely did she feel the rôle that, notwithstanding she had danced it scores of times, the end of the ballet invariably found her physically and mentally exhausted. Certain moments in her performance still persist in my memory, particularly the manner in which she toyed with the sword during the mad scene—her childlike delight in the flashing blade and then her sudden realisation of its ability to remove her from a world of woe. Then there was that awe-inspiring moment when she emerged from her tomb and slowly changed from cold clay to an intangible phantom, released from its useless envelope almost as a moth emerges from its chrysalis.

Spessivtzeva's *développés* and *arabesques* were poems of movement, and in the second act she attained a unique sense of fragility and spirituality. Markova's interpretation is remarkable for its grace and poetry and its technical beauty, so that the most difficult movements seem effortless. Her portrait of the peasant girl, like that of Spessivtzeva, has that delicately balanced hypersensitive quality so rarely encountered, while in the second act Markova is so light, so intangible, so seemingly indifferent to the laws of gravity, that she resembles a wreath of mist.

Dancers of this quality are the very personification of the romantic era, of the *femme fatale*, that elusive, fascinating, mocking vision, half woman, half goddess, which haunted the imaginations of so many poets, painters, writers, and musicians of the last century, and, becoming their muse, inspired some to achieve masterpieces.

When a group of dancers presenting *Giselle* is led by artists such as the select few I have mentioned, something of their sacred fire and of their divine magic is communicated to each and every member of the company. Then it is possible for the performance to become elevated to the height of pure poetry, and *Giselle* reasserts and maintains its claim to be regarded as the crowning glory, the supreme achievement, of the Romantic Ballet.

THE END

INDEX

135

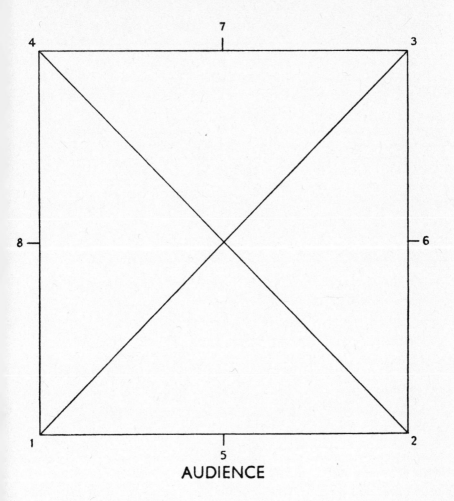

AUDIENCE